teens
@ the library
series

More Teen Programs
that work

RoseMary
Honnold

BIBLIOTHÈQUES
uOttawa
LIBRARIES

Neal-Schuman Publishers, Inc.

New York   London

b30483876

 **Don't miss the companion Web site that accompanies this book! See preface for details! Visit www.cplrmh.com/moreteenprograms.html to easily visit the Internet resources. The links will be updated periodically to keep the resources current.**

Z
718.5
.M59
2005

Published by Neal-Schuman Publishers, Inc.
100 William Street, Suite 2004
New York, NY 10038

Printed and bound in the United States of America.

The paper used in this publication meets the minimum requirements of American National Standard for Information Sciences—Permanence of Paper for Printed Library Materials, ANSI Z39.48—1992. ∞

Library of Congress Cataloging-in-Publication Data

More teen programs that work / edited by RoseMary Honnold.
    p. cm. — (Teens @ the library series)
    Includes bibliographical references and index.
    ISBN 1-55570-529-4 (alk. paper)
    1. Young adults' libraries—Activity programs—United States. 2. Libraries and teenagers—United States. 3. Teenagers—Books and reading—United States.
I. Honnold, RoseMary, 1954- II. Series.

Z718.5.M59 2005
027.62'6—dc22

                                     2004019032

Dedicated to the memory of my niece
Keely Jo Maxwell
1987–2004

Contents

Figures List

Series Editor's Foreword

Joel Shoemaker

Got teens? Sure, that's reason enough to be happy. It means you're doing things right. You've created an attractive and functional space, stocked an eclectic and challenging collection, made the young adults in your community feel welcome and . . . now, sometimes, you feel you could use some help with ideas about how to entice more new teens to come to the library, or how to get those teens to do more, be more, or think more once they are on site. RoseMary Honnold is here with enough great real-world, teen-tested ideas to enable you to 1) offer your Teen Advisory Board a list of eight ideas to choose from per month for a year and still have plenty left over or 2) introduce a new idea to your newest 13-year-old TAB member and keep him/her supplied with one new idea per month until they are no longer a teenager and still have some more great ideas left over. In other words, this book is chock full of activities, programs, and other ideas that you can use to help the teens in your community grow and learn—and have fun while doing it. Many of these program ideas will no doubt inspire you to generate you own adaptations based on the needs of your teens, your library and your community. Inspired programming and promotions will strengthen and add real value to the work you do to help teens succeed.

Like all the books in the teens @ the library series, *More Teen Programs That Work*

- Draws from the best, most current research,
- Targets the changing needs of today's teenagers,
- Cites the most innovative models,
- Provides practical suggestions that have been real-world tested, and
- Calls on each of us to realize the highest ideals of our profession.

Take these ideas and run with it. Run to your Teen Advisory Board, run to your young adult customers, run to your professional colleagues, run to your community, and keep on running with these ideas about ways to involve your teens in safe, rewarding, and fun experiences that will help them continue to develop the skills, attitudes, and behaviors they need to succeed. And if, after a few years, you run out of ideas from this book? Go back to the original book, *101+ Teen Programs That Work*, and start reading through again. You're sure to find programs and activities to motivate and inspire.

Preface

**The question:
Are there 101 MORE teen programs that work?
The answer:
Yes!**

More Teen Programs That Work follows in the footsteps of *101+ Teen Programs That Work*. It contains programs that have been collected from creative young adult librarians all across the country. These educational and entertaining events can be produced even in times of restricted library budgets, reduced staff, and tightened schedules.

Each idea in *More Teen Programs That Work* includes detailed instructions that will help first-time and experienced programmers successfully deliver. Photos, sample handouts, and other tips are included to give a full sense of the programs. Each activity includes a Collection Connection, to help librarians incorporate books, magazines, and other library materials. Finally, because it is important to provide teens with programs that stimulate them and solicit positive responses, Teen Feedback sections follow each program. These responses were provided by the librarians who submitted the programs and are proof positive that these programs do work!

The programs in this book are designed to be both fun and educational. Most, if not all, steer teens to books and other library materials and services. Most important, they are included to help build sound relationships—among teens, between YA librarians and their audience, and between teens and the library.

Chapter 1, "Measuring Unmeasurable Outcomes," inspires librarians to develop effective teen programs. This chapter outlines the measurable outcomes the programs produce—outcomes that contribute to the Search Institute's list of assets that help young people become caring, responsible adults. This chapter also includes an essay "On Libraries" by library student Mamie Alsdurf, who tells us the role a library can play in the life of a teen.

Chapter 2 contains five programs that coincide with summer reading programs and Teen Read Week. Much more than reading groups, this batch uses everything from pop culture to travel to get teens interested in reading.

Chapter 3 collects four independent programs. These can be hosted throughout the year and can often be developed into ongoing programs that teens can participate in at their leisure. Perfect for busy librarians and an elusive teen audience, they are fast, easy, cheap, and, most importantly, fun.

Chapter 4 introduces nearly 30 new craft programs, because librarians realize that crafts are among the most popular events for teens. These ideas utilize all types of media, from glass to paper to tattoos.

Chapter 5 compiles 13 book-themed programs. Each one draws a connection to a specific genre, format, or title.

Chapter 6 understands that the true way to a teen's heart is through the stomach and provides programs that will entice—and sometimes test (Fear Factor anyone?)—taste buds. Everyone says "If you feed them, they will come!" and these programs are sure to prove that point.

Because teens are always up for a good party, a fun game, or even a lock-in, Chapter 7 features eight ideas to satisfy their needs. Each of the suggestions can be adapted to meet your library's staff and budget considerations.

Chapters 8, 9, and 10 will help you plan for specific groups—girls, boys, and tweens. These chapters focus on their specific interests and needs and give tips for spending quality time with each group.

Chapter 11 has ideas for getting teens to interact with adults and with children. Getting different generations working, playing, and learning together produces both an enjoyable time and a double service for your library community.

Chapter 12 offers writing programs that can be hosted as one-time events or combined into an ongoing series. Good writing skills will not only help teens do well in school but will also be personally satisfying.

Chapter 13 shares several ways to give teens the opportunity to showcase their talents and build their confidence. Put the spotlight on your teens and watch them shine!

Chapter 14 builds both educational skills and life skills through programs. These activities offer an exciting and effective way to deliver valuable lessons to young adults.

Chapter 15 shows how teens can contribute to the mission and goals of libraries. Teens are great volunteers, *if* they are motivated and aware of their purpose. For teens and librarians, these are worthwhile investments with results that you can see.

The questionnaire that I sent to the contributors is printed in Appendix A and the list of the amazing, creative, and generous YA librarians who contributed their successful programs to this collection appears in Appendix B.

All services take some amount of time, effort, and money, but luckily for young adult librarians, this work is also fun and personally rewarding. The programs in this book were sent to me not only because the teens enjoyed them, but because the librarians who presented them did too!

Lastly, if you want to know if these programs will work for your teens, just ask them! Take a few of these ideas to your teen advisory board or conduct a survey of the teens hanging around in your library and see which programs interest them. Then put them to work helping to make it happen!

Acknowledgments

Thank you to

Charles Harmon, the director of publishing at Neal-Schuman, for giving me the opportunity to write this book.

Michael Kelley, my editor, for his support, encouragement, and editorial expertise.

Patrick Jones, mentor and colleague, for suggesting I write this book.

The contributors for their generosity and willingness to share their great ideas.

My husband, family, and friends for cheering me on.

Introduction

Patrick Jones
(Coauthor of *Connecting Young Adults*
***and Libraries*, Neal-Schuman, 2004)**

No one entered the library profession to sign up people for computers, to quiet cell-phone conversations, or to put paper in printers, yet why does that seem to make up the bulk of our work in public libraries? In school libraries, no one became a school librarian to write passes, fix every teacher's computer problem ("hmm, is it plugged in?"), or be the last-minute substitute teacher who never actually gets to teach. So, why do we do this work?

Because we want to make a difference in the lives of young people. And no two young people need or want the same things—from libraries or for their lives. Adolescence is a journey, and sometimes a teen pulls over to spend some time with us. Some want merely to read, to study, to be left alone; some want to surf, print, read, print some more, chat a little, listen to music, download a file (all this at the same time); and some teens, with a tip of the hat to the queen of the Rock and Wrestling Connection circa 1984 Cindi Lauper, just want to have fun.

And that's where programming comes in and produces outcomes for teens. Real outcomes: not just clapping their hands at the end of a clown show, but real outcomes as they learn a skill, show off a talent, test their knowledge, and learn to work and play with others. In the teen world, fun rather than fundamental life skills is an easier sell. So, bring 'em in with any of these program ideas, but know they might leave with more than a smile on their face, especially if you plan programs around building developmental assets. You could take any of these programs, or the ones you plan and produce, and evaluate them by the numbers. Not just the number that attends, but by the number of assets you can build in teens.

Of course, what you build depends upon the capacity of your organization, the needs of your community, your level of youth involvement, and your own likes and dislikes. Many of these programs will work for you, others won't. They provide models to build upon and ideas to inspire—and they may even make you think, "I should have thought of that!" or "We've got to try that!" The skills that make us good customer service librarians with youth also help us in programming: patience, persistence, and perspective. Not everything works or works right away, and if it doesn't, it's not the end of the world; you should still feel fine, and a little smarter.

RoseMary is generous not only with her time, but also with her talents as a connector of people and program ideas from across the nation. But there's more—so much more. If you program, take time to write up your programs and share them with others. The vehicles are numerous:

- Share on any of the Young Adult Library Services Association electronic lists such as YALSA-BK (for programs related to promoting reading), YAL-OUT (for outreach programs), or YA-YAAC (for programs related to youth involvement).
- Apply for awards such as the Sagebrush Award for a Young Adult Reading or Literature Program.
- Submit your Teen Read Week program to YALSA.
- Share ideas on state, regional, or even local listservs.
- Attend and present at ALA, PLA, and state conferences.
- Encourage your state youth consultants (where available) to publish a teen section of the state summer reading program manual.

Maybe you are the shy type and don't wish to share; there are many ways to explore teen programs once you've digested those that RoseMary has provided:

- Visit YALSA's professional development center, in particular the Web site on programming: www.ala.org/ala/yalsa/profdev/programming young.htm.
- Visit other young adult library Web sites. An index is available at Tracey Firestone's Virtual YA: http://yahelp.suffolk.lib.ny.us/virtual.html.
- Do a search at http://news.google.com/ with the term "young adult program" to gather from local news sources great things happening around the country.

The ideas for teen programming are endless and dynamic.

Most every teen librarian could tell you tales of programs that were hits (good turnout, better outcomes), misses (bad turnout, worse outcomes), and dogs (you consider working at Wal-Mart before the program is over). Thankfully, lots of librarians have shared with RoseMary, who now shares with you, programs that really work. From the Anime Teen Club to Pizza and Politicians, these programs showcase teen librarians with talent, a touch for the creative, and an understanding—based on involvement, intuition, and experience—of real teen needs. This book is all about librarians doing more than getting it right. Indeed, these programs show librarians changing teens' lives, one program at a time.

Chapter 1

Measuring
Unmeasurable Outcomes

Looking for measurable outcomes? Are you asked to prove that programming for teens is worthwhile before you can even try one? Are you at a loss trying to compare YA statistics with the Children's Department to make your case for teen programming?

Young adult librarians are special people. We want to share our love of reading, libraries, and books with teenagers, who many would say are the toughest audience. We've learned that a good program will bring teens to the library; we are challenged to continue producing programs that will keep our busy, ever changing audience coming back.

We have learned from the Search Institute that teens need to build as many of the Forty Developmental Assets as they can to become healthy, productive adults. The more assets teens have, the less likely they are to engage in negative behaviors and the more likely they are to engage in positive behaviors. The Search Institute tells us that relationships are key and if we think of our own teen years, this rings true.

Most adults who have done well in life can remember at least one special person who gave them opportunities to build some of these assets. While parents usually provide many of life's needs and comforts, the other adults helped us build a true perspective of our place in the world. It is how the world outside our families welcomes us, nurtures us, and guides us that helps us find our place in society. If you are reading this book, you were one of the lucky kids who had a chance because an adult took an interest in you, provided guidance and opportunities, and was a role model for you. Who turned you on to reading and books and libraries? How has that love shaped your life?

Libraries can be a significant part of a teen's life as a source of informational and recreational reading, of course, but also a place of active learning, safe exploration, and entertainment with peers and other adults. Young adult librarians are complementing the work of teachers, coaches, youth group leaders, scout leaders, and others who invest their energies into helping teens build assets. Teens who haven't found their talents and strengths yet and aren't joining teams and clubs at school can still find a place at the library, where everyone has a right to information and access to programs and there should be no social barriers.

Thanks to the excellent creations of today's young adult authors, libraries can have hip and relevant collections of reading, listening, and viewing materials for teens. Libraries are planning amazing spaces for these collections, designed specifically to appeal to teens, and multimedia centers with technology I hadn't dreamed of when I was a teen. Young adult librarians are hired to motivate the teens to use these new spaces and materials, and programming is a great way to bring it all together. Libraries offering programs that give teens opportunities to build the Forty Developmental Assets are investing in the future of the teens, of libraries, and of communities.

A teen who is turned on to libraries and books, who had a chance to learn something new, who met a new friend, who began to built an asset . . . that's the measurable outcome we are looking for when working with young people in libraries. After you read this book and try these programs . . . many more teens will be building assets in *your* library.

Mamie, the "wannabe" librarian in *101+ Teen Programs that Work*, is now a library student. I asked her to write about the role the library has played in her life.

ON LIBRARIES, BY MAMIE ALSDURF

It was their smell that drew me in. The deep, rustic aroma of books with yellowing pages. I knew right then that I would spend the rest of my life surrounded by their presence, helping others to see the beauty and knowledge the pages possess. I was nine years old. And more than anything in the world, I wanted to be a librarian.

Throughout the past eleven years, I have held that same ambition close to my heart. From elementary school recesses spent helping the librarian laminate paperback novels to long, lingering Sundays spent tucked away in the shelves, eyes glued to a book, I have found a haven in words. It is the words that jump out from the page, holding on to a reader long after the book has been returned, that captures the power of literature for me.

Volunteering at my public library throughout my high school years, I was shown first hand what impact public libraries can have on individuals, particularly teens. Even those who hated to read would spend hours browsing the shelves, filling out word puzzles, and participating in YA programming. Weekday afternoons, the YA section would be bustling with kids reading magazines, working on homework, or searching the shelves for wisdom or answers to questions they thought they couldn't ask. The library acts as a place not only to gather information for school-related topics, but also to gather information on life. The teens would come for friendship, community, and refuge—myself included. When I was faced with moving across the country at thirteen, going into a strange town not knowing a soul, I found peace at the library. The books, their infinite wisdom hidden behind leather-bound covers, soothed my pain and confusion. I joined the Young Adult Advisory Board, helped with children's programming and made friends with other kids who knew what it meant to love the library. It was there that I thrived.

My experience on the Coshocton Public Library's Teen Advisory Board (TAB) reinforced my desires and my understanding of the importance of Young Adult literature and YA Programming. When given the opportunity to accompany a librarian to a conference on YA Literature, I heard authors talk about their experiences writing YA novels, why they had such a strong desire to write this genre, and I saw rooms crowded with librarians, all listening with attentive ears, eager to find ways to encourage and support the teens at their libraries. It was a great opportunity for me, one which I would not have been afforded if not for the wonderful organizations at public libraries.

Public libraries are not simply a gathering of books. They are the faces behind the books. They are self-esteem boosters, character builders, childhood memories, and lifelong friends. They are smiles on the faces of youth whose lives they've touched. And more than anything, I want to be a part of that. I feel that books, knowledge, and technology go hand in hand in creating a successful and prosperous future. The public library and the librarians I have met have changed my life in such a positive way; there is no question that I want to do the same for our future generation.

Teens need their space. They need their own space, a place to feel comfortable, relaxed, and truly at home. This is no exception when it comes to libraries. Without a separate Young Adult section, these teenagers would be shuffled between the babyish feel of the children's department and the overwhelming sensation of being a part of the adult section. The confusion that is felt during adolescence would only be intensified and the search for identity would get lost when spending too much time searching for an appropriate book.

People sometimes search all their lives to find passion. I am lucky enough to have found passion at such an early age. And I am even luckier to be able to use my passion in a positive way. Being only slightly older than a teen myself, I am at a peak point in my professional ambitions. I know what teenage angst really means. I was there. I experienced it. And I want to use that experience to help the teens of today. Libraries are my classrooms and the teenagers I meet there, my students. Not only do I want to be a librarian, but I also want to teach and show my students the wisdom behind the words of the world.

Chapter 2

Summer Reading and Teen Read Week Programs

OVERVIEW

Recently, Long Island YA librarian Ed Goldberg asked a question on a discussion list: "Why have a Summer Reading Program?" His responses from YA librarians on the list ranged from the altruistic desire to keep teens reading so they will do better in school the following year to the purely decadent excuse: they are fun! Summer Reading Programs are attractive. The displays, decorations, and program publicity send out the message that something good is going on at the library, and that brings people in. Your job is to make sure something good does happen so your teens will want to come back. Our goal is to foster lifetime readers and library users—because we know reading helps us in so many areas of life.

A Summer Reading Program is a great opportunity to start library programming for teens. Teens have more free time in the summer to come to the library and read the just-for-fun collections they don't have time for during the school year. Summer is more relaxed so it is a great time to get to know your audience a little better and show teens a good time at the library.

While a theme isn't necessary for a summer reading program, a new theme each year will have you thinking about different parts of the collection you can feature. New and different program ideas, decorations, and displays will keep your programs fresh for the teens each year. If you are wearing two hats, as children's and young adult librarian, you can use the same theme as the children's department, as long as you step it up a bit to appeal to teens by giving it a jazzier title, making it more challenging, and offering age-appropriate prizes. Successful programs from the contributors in this chapter will get you charged and thinking of all the possibilities for great programs at your library. Many of these exciting programs will attract teens any time of year.

Teen Read Week, a celebration of teens and reading in October each year, is sponsored by the American Library Association. Teen Read Week comes at a busy time of year for teens but it also comes with lots of publicity and support from Young Adult Library Services Association (YALSA). Themes, publicity materials, and program ideas are available at the YALSA Web site. Even if you can't get the teens into the library that week, take the opportunity during this time to showcase with displays and photos what you have done with the teens all year. Step out of the library and into the classroom to let the students know there is a celebration going on just for them!

TREASURE STRIPS, BY JOANNE COKER

Treasure Strips is program to reward visits to the library. Make bookmark strips from card stock and divide each into eight sections for the eight weeks of summer reading. A teen receives a strip when he registers for the Summer Reading Program (SRP). Every week he visits the library, he can ask a librarian to stamp the strip. Provide a candy jar full of mini candy bars with some of the bars marked with stickers or dots. Each time the strip is stamped, the teen reaches into the candy jar. If he chooses a candy bar with a sticker, he is an instant winner. The suggested prizes are $2.00, $5.00, or big candy bars. With four or more stamps, the strips could be entered into a grand prize drawing for $50.00 at the end of the program.

The Bottom Line

Prizes are your main expense: 350–400 small candy bars, 60 larger candy bars, and $31.00 in cash prizes for a total of $135.00–150.00.

BOOKS AND TENNIS FOR LIFE, BY ELISE SHEPPARD

This program takes advantage of something some libraries see as a liability— there is a high school next door! Elise, an avid tennis player herself, saw the potential for a perfect partnership. If your library has a tennis court, a basketball court, or other sports facility nearby, this program would work well for you. Promote the program by visiting area schools to do a tennis demonstration with the teens and to talk about summer reading.

Books and Tennis for Life requires collaboration between the library, the tennis academy, and the school. Establish communication well in advance of your program to coordinate all of the players in this team effort. The funding for this program was provided through a grant received by the tennis academy.

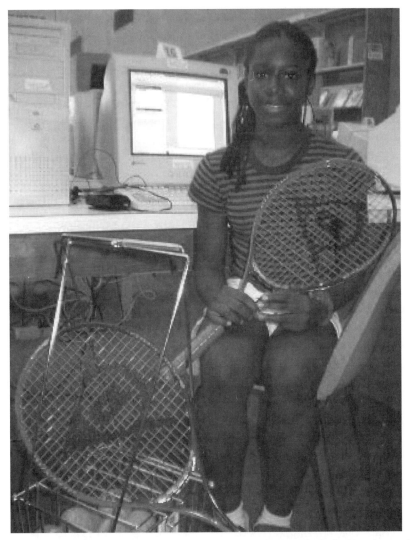

Figure 2.1 Teens exercise their bodies and their minds in Books and Tennis for Life, a sports program at the library.

Middle and high school readers learn how important it is to exercise both the mind and the body to foster a healthy lifestyle. The library provides the literacy and computer components, and the tennis academy provides professional on-court instruction and racquets for the teens to use on the courts. In order to participate in the free tennis program, teens are required to get a library card and to take part in the library's Summer Reading Program. The tennis portion of this program was held three days a week through June and

July. Parents signed a medical release form to give their child permission to participate.

The Collection Connection

When you are having a tennis, basketball, or other sports-related program, make sure your collection has new and relevant titles about the sport. Not only books about how to play the sport, but biographies of popular players and past famous players and publications on popular and local teams will also appeal to new readers who were attracted to the sports theme of the program. Display and promote novels about sports, too.

The Bottom Line

The first summer was funded with a $10,000 grant for eight tennis teaching professionals, tennis balls, tennis racquets, ice, and water containers. The second summer was funded with a $5,000 grant, and three tennis teaching professionals were employed. The tennis courts were provided rent-free through an arrangement with the high school. The library's expenses included the purchase of additional tennis books for the collection, as well as paper and copying charges for application forms, fliers, and certificates of completion for each participant.

Teen Feedback

The teens said the tennis/library program was the best part of their summer, because it was fun, it gave them something to do besides staying home and watching TV, and it was a new experience.

CSI @ THE LIBRARY, BY CHRIS HOLT

CSI @ the Library ties in with the popularity of the crime-solving television series. Chris arranged this program as one of a series of summer programs held on Friday afternoons. CSI @ the Library lasted about three hours.

The Lab Director of the coroner's office launched the program with a 45-minute Power Point presentation with questions from the audience. He touched on all the basics of the department and the differences between real life and *CSI* on TV. He displayed catalogs with the equipment they use in the lab. Chris reported that their local coroner's office was very cooperative and was accustomed to making school visits. Contact your local coroner's office or police department to inquire about a similar presentation.

Follow the presentation with a teen murder mystery game. Popular and easy to host are the Anyone's Guess Interactive Mystery Series available at www.highsmith.com and the How To Host A Teen Mystery Games available at www.mystery-games.com, but any teen murder mystery game would work. Provide a prize for the winner of the game. End the program with food and social time. Chris served pizza and pop.

Collection Connection

Display books on crime scene investigations, true crime, and law enforcement careers. Add mystery novels and movies to include the fiction collection.

The Bottom Line

Chris budgeted wisely! The presentation was free. The mystery kit was purchased a few years ago by the library system for unlimited use. Our regional library association shares our mystery kits. Mystery kits cost between $30.00 and $40.00. The pizza and beverages cost about $45.00. The prize for the mystery game was donated by a local business.

Teen Feedback

The teens' reaction was very positive. The presentation by the coroner's office was not as interactive as the murder mystery, but all 33 teens had a great time!

JOURNEY TO JAPAN AND INVITATION TO IRELAND, BY LOLA H. TEUBERT

These programs invite teens to take a week-long virtual trip to another culture. Lola arranged these cultural celebrations of Teen Read Week with a series of programs featuring Japan and Ireland. Each day a program with a cultural flair was offered after school.

Lola invited local talent for these programs and offered a small honorarium to each presenter. The programs were publicized through posters, bookmarks, radio, and TV. A series of programs can feature any culture of interest to your teens and community. Music, dance, travelogues, crafts, and food will give your teens a peek into another culture.

The Journey to Japan series included:

- Monday: Anime films.
- Tuesday: A Japanese-American high school teacher talked about living in Japan.
- Wednesday: Teens invited to try sushi, catered by a local Japanese restaurant.
- Thursday: Teens learned Japanese phrases from a teacher.
- Friday: More anime films.

The Invitation to Ireland included:

- Monday: Music of Ireland. The head of the music department at the University of Evansville sang Irish melodies accompanied by a Celtic harpist and a guitarist.
- Wednesday: Travels in Ireland. A local priest spoke about his trips to Ireland with an amusing twist.
- Friday: Irish Dance. A dance company demonstrated Irish step dancing.

This is an interesting way to let teens experience different parts of a foreign culture. Start with your speaker. Do you have someone on staff, a patron, or a schoolteacher who has immigrated to the U.S. or traveled extensively and would like to talk about it to teens? Add music, food, crafts, films, and any other suggestions your speaker may have for developing programs for the rest of the week!

The Collection Connection

Display and promote cultural music and movies, travel videos and books, maps, foreign cookery, and novels set in the featured culture.

The Bottom Line

The only expense Lola had for the Japanese program was for sushi catered by a Japanese restaurant. The Irish program included small honorariums for the speakers.

Teen Feedback

"Do Japan again!"

CAMP CREATE, BY HEATHER MILLER

Two four-day camps are the creative collaboration between Heather's library and the Birmingham Museum of Art. Brochures are sent to area schools in the spring and registration begins May 1 for teens in the sixth through twelfth grades.

One camp is literary and one is artistic and leaders are hired for each. For example, the literary camp might be about storytelling with a local storyteller as the camp leader. Teens meet with the storyteller Monday through Thursday for three hours each day and learn how to choose, memorize, and energize their stories. They learn public oratory skills needed to communicate their stories to an audience and what to do if they forget their lines while performing. The finale of the week is a performance on Thursday night for parents, siblings, and the public.

Figure 2.2 The Camp Create promotional flyer.

**Figure 2.3 Teens get a chance to explore
their artistic talents at Camp Create.**

For the artistic camp, an artist hired by the museum is the camp leader. Local well-known artists are good choices. The first day of the camp is held at the library and the following three days are at the museum in the educational complex. For the Folk Art camp, teens had four days of folk art instruction and made spirit sticks, face jugs, pizza quilts, poster-board mosaics, sandstone sculptures, painted furniture, and plywood people. Display the teens' artwork in the library and invite the teens, families, and public for an opening and reception as a finale at the end of the week.

The Bottom Line

The storyteller who led the literary camp cost $800.00, and the museum paid for the art camp leader. Snacks, drinks, writing supplies, and receptions cost $200–300 and were funded by the Friends of the Library.

The Collection Connection

Books from the library's collection for the camp topics should be on display, so teens can learn more about the arts they are studying at the camps. Camp leaders can further encourage teens to read as a follow-up by explaining how much of their training came from books and how they use them for reference in their work.

Teen Feedback

Teens often went to the YA department of the library to check out books on things they had just talked about or learned about that day at camp. The teens and their families are very complimentary about these programs. One mother said that the storytelling sessions were very good for her son because "It's taught him not to mumble and he speaks more clearly now." Another mother said, about the same program, "Carrie has had such a wonderful time this week. This creative outlet has been so much fun for her." The public also enjoyed the artwork from the camp that was displayed at the library.

Chapter 3

More Independent Programs

OVERVIEW

Independent programs are projects, games, and contests available in the young adult room for whenever teens come into the library. These programs work because they are easy and fast to put together for a busy librarian, are not victim to a teen's busy and unpredictable schedule, and are cheap to make, many requiring only a drawing box and entry slips. The only investment will be for prizes, and you can be as thrifty or as extravagant as your budget allows.

The teens on your Advisory Board may enjoy working on creating these programs and choosing prizes from catalogs. The independent programs are all designed to attract teens to the library's collection and resources. They can be used to promote social programs or a new service, be an ongoing presence in the young adult room, or pop up during holidays. Sometimes scheduling a program seems impossible for you or your teens, so put together one of these independent programs. When time and budget are tight, think *inside* the box!

WORST BOOK AWARD, BY JENNIFER STENCEL

Cover tabletops with butcher paper and set out crayons. Invite teens to write down the worst book they ever read. Jennifer uses this idea when she visits schools to entice students to come to her table. The Top Ten Worst Books list is posted at the end of the program. A teen came up with the award for the Worst Book: plant a small tree to replace all the paper used to publish the book!

GET CARDED AT THE LIBRARY DAY,
BY JENNIFER STENCEL

A library card campaign targeting teens, Get Carded rewards teens who show you their library cards. A tempting goodie box of candy or small prizes will motivate teens to get their cards replaced, renewed, and reactivated. Jennifer notes that she waives fines on cards for this program, although you could offer a list of volunteer projects so teens could work to pay off their fines. This program is a good way to launch summer reading and Teen Read Week.

TEEN CHOICE AWARDS, BY JENNIFER STENCEL

Create ballots for teens to vote for their favorites from the Grammy or Oscar nominees. List popular performers in categories on entry forms:

- Choice Movie Actor
- Choice Male Artist/Band
- Choice TV Actor
- Choice Movie Actress
- Choice Female Artist/Band
- Choice TV Actress
- Choice Movie
- Choice Album
- Choice TV Show

Include space for teen's name and phone number. The results will give you ideas for additions to the YA collection. Jennifer gave teens who completed the ballot a small prize.

THE PINK FLAMINGO HUNT, BY SANDRA LANG

A stuffed hot pink flamingo is the Summer Reading Club mascot at Sandra's library. Sandra and her husband went around town and photographed the flamingo at different places—sitting on the counter of Domino's and sitting on a park bench next to a war memorial, for example. There is always something in the picture that is not too obvious, but does allow teens to guess the flamingo's location. A different picture is posted each week of summer reading. The teens write their guesses on entry slips with their names and phone numbers. A prize winner is drawn from the correct entries. The prize sponsors liked having the flamingo photographed at their businesses.

The local school mascot or any mascot chosen by your TAB can be used for this program. Depending on the mascot, it could be photographed holding a book.

Figure 3.1 The Pink Flamingo visits a local pizza shop.

Figure 3.2 The Pink Flamingo relaxes in the park.

Chapter 4

More Craft Programs

OVERVIEW

Teens love crafts where they can be creative and freely explore the possibilities of the medium. The easier crafts that take less time for preparation and cleanup are perfect for after-school activities. Saturdays and lock-ins are good times to tackle the crafts that may be messy or take longer to complete. Many crafts can be adapted to be included in a summer reading program for almost any theme.

You may find the materials for many of these projects already in your library's supplies or stashed away in your own home. Ask coworkers and friends to contribute their leftover craft materials to start your own collection of ready supplies or post in the staff room a wish list of supplies for specific projects. Cruise the sale tables of craft stores like JoAnn's or Michael's and close-out stores to find additional supplies at a very reasonable price.

Try out a craft before you present it to the teens. Use your prototypes in a display to promote the program so the teens can see what they can make. If you have gallery space in your library or a large display case, show off the teens' work after the program. Your library's collection and the Internet provide a vast array of project suggestions, instructions, and resources. Remember to include the craft books, videos, and software from your collection in displays. Making crafts together gives you and your teens time to spend together learning, having fun, socializing, creating, and being productive.

It doesn't matter if the turnout for a craft program is small. Often, teens will talk more and open up in a small group because they are more comfortable with their hands occupied by a project. Smaller crafts can be set up right in the young adult area as a make-it-and-take-it after-school project. I set things up, start a project, and when a teen cruises by, I show what I am working on and say, "We're making folding scrapbooks (for example) today. Want

to give it a try?" Nearly all the teens—boys and girls—stop to see what is
going on and choose to make something. If it is a project that requires drying time or setting-up time, all the better; they can browse for books while
waiting. Included in this chapter are some of the many creative projects, big
and small (or should I say messy and neat?), that have worked in libraries in
the past and you can try with your teens.

PAINT THE LIBRARY RED, WHITE, AND BLUE, BY BRIAN SIMONS

Teens and parents get involved decorating the whole library for a patriotic
July with this painting program. The plan is to paint all the library windows
with patriotic symbols such as eagles, stars, fireworks, or flags in honor of
Independence Day. This project sends a wonderful message to the community as they watch the teens and parents at work and view their artwork for
the next two weeks. The time suggestions in this program description are
based on Brian's library, which takes up a full city block. Three staff members supervise 140 painters, half of whom are teens.

This program requires staff members to be present for four or five hours
on painting day, but the painters are present for only about two hours. On
the Monday before July 4 at 10 a.m., the teens and parents meet in the library garage. The staff announces that inappropriate images or words will
not be tolerated, but Brian suggests a sense of humor when addressing this
issue: "'You know what we mean,' is usually what we say." Brian and the staff
try to use humor in order not to kill the mood.

A large cart is useful for loading all the tempera paint, brushes, rags, and
buckets for water. Move the loaded cart and the hoses that connect to the
building's outside faucets to the first area of windows to be painted. Three
library staff members can fill disposable cups or bowls with the color of tempera paint requested by each artist or team of artists and provide one-inch
foam brushes. The staff members will stay busy keeping up with color requests and cleaning brushes in the water. As the window space is filled on
one side of the library, move the cart and hoses so the teens and parents can
work their way around the building. Once the painting is finished about two
hours later, the staff and volunteers can go around and wash off any spills
on the non-glass portion of the windows, which may take another two hours.

About two weeks later, the three library staff members and volunteers clean
off the windows with hot, soapy water, a brush, and a hose. The clean-up
session may take three to four hours, depending on the size of your windows
and the number of people working.

Brian announces Paint the Library Red, White, and Blue through program calendars, YA events brochures, signs, and flyers posted at teen-fre-

Figure 4.1 Miss Liberty strikes a pose on the window of Brian's library, thanks to this artistic teen.

Figure 4.2 Teams of teens and parents work together during Paint the Library Red, White, and Blue.

quented businesses, and Public Service Announcements (PSA). Brian also uses an e-mail list for teens who sign up for summer reading.

The Bottom Line

The cost for this project was staff salaries plus paint and brushes, which cost about $160.00. Expenses for your project will be less or more, depending on the window space you have available to paint. If you want to try this project on a much smaller scale, invite TAB members to paint designs on the glass doors or windows of the library entrance for any holiday occasion or to decorate the YA room windows with any book images or characters.

Teen Feedback

Brian reports that the teens love this program and respond with a lot of positive feedback: "Thanks, this was so much fun." "We should do this for all the holidays!"

CRAFT DAY, BY CATHY HOCHADEL

A parent of one of Cathy's teens kept offering to teach a cross-stitch class. That offer ballooned into an extravagant event that was very inexpensive, fun, and rewarding. Cathy partnered with the Children's Librarian to present the program for Tweens. Patrons from their library volunteered time and materials to teach various crafts in one- or one-and-a-half-hour program increments offered throughout the day. Since two or three of the instructors volunteered to supply their own materials, it was only fair that all the instructors provide their own materials.

To solicit instructors for a craft day, post a sign describing the program and asking for adult volunteer instructors; take the names, craft name, and phone numbers of adults offering their services. One month before the event, confirm the instructors and set up the class schedule. Three weeks before the program, devise and post the class schedule so kids can sign up for the classes. Preregistration is necessary so instructors can bring enough supplies. Ask the instructors to bring in samples of their craft, so they can be on display in case teens are unfamiliar with the craft. Three days before the class, tally the number of participants each instructor will have; call the instructors and advise them. Two days before the class, call the participants and remind them about the classes (significant changes in class size should be reported to the instructor). One day before the program, be sure your camera is ready to go!

On the day of the event, set up tables and cover with paper, if requested. Direct tweens to the appropriate work stations; have them make name tags so the instructor can call them by name. Send a thank-you note and an evaluation form to the instructors within one week after the program.

Scissors, rulers, and extra hands to help hold things were the only things Cathy needed to contribute. She also provided stickers for name tags. They didn't serve food, but there were between five and ten kids who were there virtually all day: the next time they do this program, they will schedule a noontime break and tell kids to bring a sack lunch!

Collection Connection

Display craft books and videos so the participants can continue to learn their crafts on their own.

ECO-TRASH OR EARTH DAY ZOO, BY CATHY HOCHADEL

If this program is presented in April, it can be a great Earth Day project; however, it can be presented anytime as an environmental awareness program. Eco-trash (or Earth Day Zoo) allows teens to be imaginative, and the results of their creativity can then be used for a library display. It is fun to do this one- or one-and-a-half-hour program outside. The teens will be creating a zoo of creatures from recycled materials. Create a creature to display for promoting the program.

Prior to the program, you will need to collect trash and supplies for creating the zoo. Suggested materials are:

- Plastic 2 liter and 16 oz. bottles
- Foam trays from produce or bakery products; foam cups and bowls
- Aluminum foil, aluminum plates
- Tissue paper rolls, paper towel rolls, wrapping paper tubes
- Egg cartons
- Interestingly shaped junk
- Thread spools, corks, calculator or cash register paper roll tubes, tape roll tubes, bottle caps, jar lids, etc.

You will also need to have these items on hand: glue, glue gun, rubber bands, paper clips, clothespins, stapler, scissors, tapes (clear shipping, scotch, and masking), a utility knife, bright gold spray paint, and a large cardboard box to be used as a spray-painting booth.

On program day, set up the painting booth, sort the recycled materials, and display the tools and supplies. Teens bring their imaginations to create birds and animals from the trash collection. You will probably be asked to hold, help, balance, and tape. Glued animals will need some drying time. After the creatures are assembled and glue has been allowed to dry, coat all surfaces of the creatures with the bright gold spray paint.

The creatures can be displayed indoors or outdoors; the key is to display them where the sun will shine on them for best effect. If the display is outdoors, the creatures will last at least through the first rain storm.

Collection Connection

Display books and magazines on ecology and environmental issues.

HOT STUFF GLASS ETCHING, BY CYNTHIA GAYNOR

As part of the Hot Stuff for Cool Teens Summer Reading Program, Cynthia's library held a glass-etching workshop. Collect glass objects to etch, or purchase inexpensive drinking glasses. Purchase etching cream and stencils at a craft store. Follow the time instructions on the etching cream. Set up a series of stations for the teens to work through to complete a project:

- Check in.
- Select materials and instructions.
- Clean glass and apply stencils.
- Apply etching cream.
- Remove cream and stencil.

The Bottom Line

The etching cream is inexpensive, so this is a very cheap program if you collect glass objects rather than buy new ones. Try yard sales for inexpensive glassware.

Teen Feedback

The teens were thrilled with their projects and planned to give them as gifts.

DUCTIGAMI, BY KAREN J. DEANGELO

Duct tape crafts are great for boys and girls for a craft program after school or on a Saturday. Almost any article of clothing or container can be crafted of duct tape, which is nearly indestructible. The tape comes in several colors and even a few patterned designs and is available in hardware stores. A few Web sites and books show photos of duct tape prom dresses and tuxes where teens have entered their designs in a Stuck at Prom contest for scholarships!

Try the projects you will be offering to learn how to handle the tape and to create samples for a promotional display so the teens can see what they can make. Allow about two hours for this program to demonstrate, make a practice bookmark, and complete a small project, like a wallet, sandals, water bottle holder, picture frame, or CD case. Project instructions are available in the resources listed in the Collection Connection.

Gather rulers, yardsticks, and scissors, as well as several duct tape craft books for patterns. Permanent or paint markers and stencils or colored plastic tape are fun to use to further decorate the projects. Photocopy instructions of the projects in your display and offer the duct tape craft books for teens who want to try something on their own. Each teen will need table space to measure, rip, and assemble the projects. One staff member can assist about five or six teens.

The Bottom Line

Duct tape can be found at the dollar store, where there is less on a roll but since you need one roll per person, it can save money. More interesting colors and patterns can be purchased at hardware and department stores; check the hunting department for camouflage duct tape. Tape can also be purchased online. One large roll will make several projects; the smaller colored rolls will make one wallet each if you make no mistakes.

The Collection Connection

Berg, Jim, and Tim Nyberg. 2003. *The Original Duct Tape Halloween Book.* New York: Workman Pub.

Duck Tape Club Ductivities. Available: www.ducktapeclub.com/ducktivities. (December 2004)

Schiedermayer, Ellie. 2002. *Got Tape? Roll Out the Fun with Duct Tape.* Iola, WI: Krause.

Scotch 3M Company. Duct Tape Workshop. Available: www.3m.com/intl/CA/english/centres/home_leisure/duct_tape/dt_wallet.html. (December 2004)

Sean's Duct Tape Page Projects. Available: http://seanm.ca/duct-tape/projects.html. (December 2004)

Wilson, Joe. 1999. *Ductigami: the Art of the Tape.* Erin, Ont.: Boston Mills Press.

Teen Feedback

The teens who attended a duct tape program at Coshocton last summer were talking about their duct tape projects months later. A girl said her dad was still carrying his duct tape wallet! Some teens continued learning how to make duct tape projects from the books and Web sites.

HENNA TATTOOS, BY MELISSA PILLOT

Introduce the art of henna tattoo by explaining some of its history and cultural background. The henna plant has been used as a cosmetic and medicine for thousands of years and was originally grown in the hot, dry climates of Egypt, Australia, Asia, and the Mediterranean coast of North Africa. The first henna users may have used it as a deodorant as the paste keeps the skin from perspiring but it has also been used to treat sprains, strains, cuts, and burns. Henna art is very much like a language or secret code: in Morocco, certain Mehndi designs are used to ward off bad luck and in India, Mehndi celebrates religious occasions and ceremonies. To get the henna paste, people grind up the leaves of the henna plant and mix it with oils. The stain it leaves on the skin is caused by a chemical reaction with the keratin found in the skin.

Purchase henna kits for the program. Often, the stencils, applicators, and instructions are included with the kits. Be prepared with plenty of paper towels and wet wipes. You will also need cotton swabs, eucalyptus oil, henna applicators, henna paste, and Indian or African background music.

Teens have the option of creating their henna designs, copying one from a book, or tracing a temporary tattoo. The participants clean the area of their arms where they wish to draw the tattoo. Each participant dips a cotton swab in the eucalyptus oil and rubs it on the clean skin until the area is moist. Those using temporary tattoos should then press the tattoo firmly and flat against the skin, hold it there for one minute, and then remove the backing of the tattoo from the skin. Pass out the henna applicators so the participants may begin drawing their designs. If teens work on themselves and each other, only one staff member is needed. Volunteers are helpful if you have a large group.

Collection Connection

Beukel, Dorine van den. 2000. *Traditional Mehndi Designs: A Treasury of Henna Body Art.* Boston: Shambhala; New York: Distributed in the U.S. by Random House.

Earth Henna. Available: http://earthhenna.com (December 2004).

Fabius, Carine. 1998. *Mehndi: The Art of Henna Body Painting.* Photographs by Michele Maurin Garcia and Pascal Giacomini. 1st ed. New York: Three Rivers Press.

Ganeri, Anita. 1996. *Beliefs and Cultures: Hindu.* Danbury, Conn.: Childrens Pr; 1st Amercian ed (March 1).

Glicksman, Jane. 2000. *The Art of Mehndi.* Illustrated by Renee Trachtenberg. Los Angeles: Lowell House Juvenile.

The Henna Page. Available: www.hennapage.com (December 2004).

The Henna Tattoos People. Available: www.hennaweb.com (December 2004).

Weiss, Stefanie Iris. 1999. *Everything You Need to Know About Mendhi, Temporary Tattoos, and Other Temporary Body Art.* New York: Rosen Publishing Group; 1st ed (December 1).

The Bottom Line

A $20.00 kit will do about 40 tattoos.

Teen Feedback

Melissa says this is one of the most popular teen programs, even attracting older teens.

CREATE YOUR OWN PAPIER-MÂCHÉ CREATURE, BY LAURA VINOGRAD

Teens will be attracted to this creative two-session program by the papier-mâché samples you create for displays in the weeks leading up to the program. The whimsical figures are approximately 12" by 18" in size. Laura's samples included a colorful bird, a Cheshire cat, and a man leaning back looking skyward with a book in his lap. The teens who participated made both realistic and whimsical figures, ranging from manatees and penguins, to horses and ducks.

Prepare for this program by collecting plastic bags, newspapers, and scrap cardboard. Tear the newspapers into strips of varying widths. To make the papier-mâché paste, mix equal parts flour and water until smooth. Laura's group of 17 teens used 17 pounds of paste. Cover the floor and tables with drop cloths for easy cleanup, and provide old shirts for the teens to put over their clothes or advise them to wear old T-shirts. The paste washes out easily but the teens will get messy!

For the first session, create the basic shape of the creature by stuffing wadded newspaper into a plastic shopping bag. It should be firm but not rock hard. Then tape on cardboard tubes with masking tape to make legs and necks. More cardboard shapes can be added to make heads, feet, beaks, and tails. Once the basic shape is created, the teens dip strips of newspaper in the paste and lay all over the creature's body, overlapping strips to make two to three layers. Set up fans to dry the figures more quickly. When completely dry, approximately two days later, spray paint the figures white to provide a good base for decorating.

Invite the teens to bring feathers, felt, yarn, sequins, and other craft materials for a second night of fun painting and decorating the creatures. Provide craft paint, brushes, glue, and any available leftover craft items. The paint will dry quickly enough for the teens to take their creations home after the program. Play music in the background to set a creative, fun atmosphere.

Collection Connection

Display papier-mâché and other craft books.

The Bottom Line

The only expense is flour for the paste and paint. All other items are recycled. Use leftover craft paint from other projects to save money.

Teen Feedback

All of the teens returned for the second session and stayed for two hours of fun and laughter.

PAPERMAKING, BY AMY DOTY

Papermaking is a program that fits in well with many different themes, from a cultural program about Ancient Egypt or Ancient China, to recycling and bookmaking. Amy's teens enjoyed creating Valentines with their homemade paper in February to celebrate Library Lovers' Month. Not only is making homemade paper a fun experience for you and the teens, but it's also a good way to recycle waste into wonderful possibilities such as envelopes, greeting cards, artwork, and more.

The process will take about one-and-a-half hours, and two staff members or volunteers would be helpful. You will need:

- Fiberglass screening
- Inexpensive wood frames
- Tubs
- Blenders
- Scrap paper
- Newspapers
- Sponges
- An iron
- Rags
- A hairdryer

Prepare the area for papermaking by covering the tables and the floor with old newspapers or drop cloths. Select the pieces of paper to be recycled. You can mix different types to create your own unique paper. Rip the paper into small bits or use a paper shredder. Place the shredded paper into a blender until it is about half full and fill the blender with warm water. Run the blender slowly at first, then increase the speed until the pulp looks smooth and well blended—30 to 40 seconds. Check that no flakes of paper remain. If there are, blend longer.

The next step is to make a deckle. This is done by stretching fiberglass screening over a wooden frame and stapling it around the perimeter. It should be as tight as possible. Fill a tub about halfway with water. The tub needs to

Figure 4.3 Teens pose in front of the Library Lover's Month bulletin board featuring valentines to the library made on handmade paper.

be large enough to submerge the deckle. Add three blender loads of pulp to the tub. The more pulp you add the thicker the finished paper will be. Stir the mixture. Place the deckle into the pulp and then level it out while it is submerged, by gently wiggling the frame side-to-side until the pulp on top of the screen looks even. Slowly lift up the frame until it is above the level of the water. Wait until most of the water has drained from the new paper sheet. If the paper is very thick, use less pulp in the tub. If it is too thin, add more pulp and stir the mixture again. If you want to add glitter to the paper, sprinkle it over the wet pulp on the deckle.

When the pulp stops dripping, gently ease the deckle down flat, flipping the pulp side down on a sheet of paper, wax paper, or newspaper on the table. Use a sponge to press out as much water as possible. Wring the excess water from the sponge back into the large plastic tub. Now comes the tricky part. Slowly lift the edge of the deckle—leaving the pulp on the table surface. If it sticks to the deckle, you may have pulled too fast or not pressed out enough water. It takes a little practice. You can gently press out any bubbles and loose edges at this point.

Either let the paper dry overnight and press with an iron, just like ironing a shirt, or place in the microwave for thirty-second intervals to help it dry faster. If you used glitter, you cannot iron the paper or put it in the micro-wave. Decorate the paper, write poetry on it, or make cards or collages!

The Bottom Line

Amy bought the screening from a local hardware store for under $3.00. She purchased the frames and a couple of sponges at a "dollar store" and found everything else at home or the library.

The Collection Connection

Use and display papermaking and recycling books and any library materials that connect with the overall theme of the papermaking program.

Teen Feedback

Teens were very interested in making paper at home with their families.

VALENTINE WORKSHOP, BY IRENE SCHERER

Teens can make custom candy-bar wrappers and valentines while learning how to use graphics software. This is a fun program for the computer lab where one instructor can aid about eight teens. Irene used the Adobe Photoshop Elements software.

For the candy wrappers, provide candy bars (at least two kinds so the teens have a choice), printer paper, and a color printer. Go through the process step by step to create a sample wrapper and then let the teens design their own. After designing a wrapper, print it out, trim it to fit a candy bar, and secure it with tape.

After they make a wrapper, show the teens the steps to design valentine cards. Print the cards on card stock. The cards can be trimmed with fancy-edged scissors.

The Bottom Line

The cost of this program is determined by how many candy bars you give each teen and how many teens participate. This is an economical program that is educational, fun, and a good use for computer labs. Get comfortable with a graphics software program or ask the technology department to help you with the workshop.

Teen Feedback

Irene did the same program for a previous Valentine's Day. It had been very successful so she repeated it—registration filled up quickly and she had a wait-ing list. The teens are proud of what they made.

KNITTING FOR TEENS, BY SOPHIE BROOKOVER

Teens learn beginning knitting skills in this 90-minute workshop. For teaching first-timers, Sophie recommends using a wool-acrylic blend such as Lion Brand's Wool-Ease. Widely available in craft stores, this product comes in large, inexpensive skeins. Wool blends are much easier to learn on than cotton, which has no natural stretch to it. Wool is nice and stretchy, so it can take quite a beating and is blessedly forgiving to the novice knitter, who frequently knits very tightly. Opt for short, straight needles, because long straight needles are unwieldy.

Set up the room with a skein of yarn, a pair of needles, a crochet hook, and a take-home instruction packet at each seat. Set up a display of knitting books, videos, and software from the collection on a nearby table. Teach the teens how to cast on and do a basic knit stitch. After knitting several rows, show them how to bind off.

The instruction packet should have reminders of how to do what they just learned and instructions for doing the purl stitch. Alternatively, schedule another class to learn the purl stitch and begin a project. At about the midpoint of the program, Sophie had the teens take a break while she booktalked the materials on display. They were all checked out at the end of the program.

If you have an interested group that would like to continue knitting together, start a Teen Knitting Club. Meet weekly or monthly to learn a new knitting skill, work on projects, or listen to booktalks or audio books.

Sophie used the following Web sites as resources for instructions on the handouts:

- About.com: http://knitting.about.com. Many free patterns and stitch workshops are linked from this page.
- Basic Scarf Pattern: http://tinyurl.com/yurdr
- Better Homes & Gardens: www.bhg.com. Every month, bhg.com provides different free patterns for you to try and enjoy.
- Binding off: www.wonderful-things.com/newknit6.htm
- Casting on: www.wonderful-things.com/newknit1a.htm
- Correcting Errors: www.wonderful-things.com/newknit8.htm
- Knit Stitch: http://tinyurl.com/yttw7
- Knitty Magazine: www.knitty.com. This is a free online magazine that offers cute patterns, articles about knitting, and tips galore. Hipper than BHG, but not so trendy that their patterns will look dated next year.
- Making a Gauge Swatch: http://tinyurl.com/34vcg
- Making a Slipknot: http://tinyurl.com/27sys
- Purl Stitch: http://tinyurl.com/2zq4g

Knitting for Teens

@

Mount Laurel Library
January 29, 2003
7:30-9:00 PM

Learn the basics of knitting!

(we'll provide needles & yarn)

Create an easy scarf to take home!

**Registration for current library card holders begins
Wednesday, January 15, 2003!**

Knitting for Teens @
Mount Laurel Library
Register: 856.234.7319 x.335

Knitting for Teens @
Mount Laurel Library
Register: 856.234.7319 x.335

Knitting for Teens @
Mount Laurel Library
Register: 856.234.7319 x.335

Knitting for Teens @
Mount Laurel Library
Register: 856.234.7319 x.335

Knitting for Teens @
Mount Laurel Library
Register: 856.234.7319 x.335

Knitting for Teens @
Mount Laurel Library
Register: 856.234.7319 x.335

Knitting for Teens @
Mount Laurel Library
Register: 856.234.7319 x.335

Knitting for Teens @
Mount Laurel Library
Register: 856.234.7319 x.335

Knitting for Teens @
Mount Laurel Library
Register: 856.234.7319 x.335

Knitting for Teens @
Mount Laurel Library
Register: 856.234.7319 x.335

**Figure 4.4 Publicity posters with tear-off slips provide
contact information for the teens to take with them.**

- Substituting Yarns: http://knitting.about.com/library/weekly/
  aa022397.htm

Collection Connection

Booktalk all the knitting books and materials, and showcase helpful online
resources. All of the books were checked out at the end of the evening, and
Sophie has ordered more books on knitting for the YA collection.

The Bottom Line

The expenses include a skein of yarn and a pair of knitting needles for each teen. Friends and coworkers who knit or crochet afghans may have leftover skeins to donate.

Teen Feedback

Several of the girls had wanted to learn to knit and were happy with the program. They felt they could continue learning more based on what they had learned at the program.

IT'S A BEAD THING, BY JOAN WEISKOTTEN

When a coworker has an interesting hobby, ask her to share what she knows in a program for teens. Joan's coworker, Claudia Hayes, is an experienced beader. Claudia generously shared her time, talent, and supplies to introduce teens to beading.

To prepare a bead program, collect or purchase a variety of beads and place them in separate bowls on each table. After the teens are seated at the tables, explain the different types of materials they will be using, and demonstrate a few simple techniques for making bracelets, necklaces, and earrings. It is helpful to have samples to show and handouts of instructions for projects. The teens then choose a design and pick out the appropriate beads and cord or wire. Joan's teens were allowed to make two projects.

The materials needed for the program include beads in all different shapes, sizes, colors, and materials, as well as wire and nylon cord. You also need a few jewelry tools such as needle-nose pliers and wire cutters. Joan and Claudia required preregistration and had 18 participants.

The Bottom Line

Joan's expenses were relatively low because Claudia donated most of the beads from her own personal collection, and they used her tools.

Teen Feedback

The teens absolutely loved the program and asked when they were going to do it again.

SKETCH, BY MELISSA PILLOT

Lead middle school teens through a one-hour sketching lesson at the library. You will need an 80-page sketch book (acid-free, 50 lb. weight paper) and a pencil for each student; objects to sketch (apple, radio, globe, stuffed animal, etc.); and an overhead projector with images on transparencies to draw.

Introduce the program by asking, "How would you define the word sketch?" As the teens answer and discuss this question, pass out sketchbooks and pencils and instruct them to write their names on the inside cover. Begin the program with this warm-up exercise taken from *Drawing with Children* by Mona Brookes:

- Open sketchbooks to the first page.
- Draw four straight lines from one edge of the paper to the other.
- Draw two more straight lines from one edge of the paper to the other, only this time, make the lines cross over the lines you have already drawn.
- Draw five circles, any size, anywhere on the paper.
- Draw two curved lines beginning at the edge of the paper and ending up somewhere in the middle of the paper.

The teens can share and compare their different creations using the same instructions. The exercise helps explain that art is subjective; there is no one correct way to draw.

For the next exercise, divide the teens into four groups with one group at each table. Turn off the lights and turn on the overhead projector, showing a series of images. Ask the participants to draw the pictures they see projected, allowing three to five minutes for each drawing.

Place three or four objects on the different tables. Encourage the teens to draw the objects, drawing what they see rather than what they know. After three minutes, have the participants switch places—either to a different seat at the table or to a different table. Continue rotating until each teen has completed six to eight sketches. Following all the exercises, invite the artists to show one drawing they are particularly proud of.

Collection Connection

Bradshaw, Percy V. 1949. *The Magic of Line: a study of drawing through the ages.* London, New York: Studio Publications.

Camp, Jeffrey. 1981. *The Drawing Book,* foreword by David Hockney. 1st American ed. New York: Holt, Rinhart, and Winston.

Cirlot, Juan-Eduardo. 1972. *Picasso: Birth of a Genius.* New York: Praeger.

Galassi, Susan Grace, ed. 1997. *Picasso's One-Liners.* New York: Artisan.

Godfrey, Tony. 1990. *Drawing Today: draughtsmen in the eighties.* Oxford [England]: Phaidon; New York: Phaidon Universe.

Herrera, Hayden. 1993. *Matisse: A Portrait.* 1st ed. New York: Harcourt Brace.

Mendelowitz, Daniel M., Duane A. Wakeham, and David L. Faber. 2003. *A Guide to Drawing*, 6th ed. Belmont, CA: Thomson/Wadsworth.

The Bottom Line

Each Sketch Journal cost $2.00. Those that were not used made great prizes for Poetry Slams in the following spring.

CHINESE JUGGLING STICKS, BY MELISSA PILLOT

This is a fun and interesting craft project for a cultural or historical program. Talk about the history and interesting facts about juggling, specifically Chinese juggling. Discuss the presence of juggling in different cultures, using the Collection Connection as resources. Chinese juggling sticks, dating back more than 3,000 years to the Shang Dynasty, are often identified as the origin of juggling. The oldest representations or documentation of juggling were discovered on the wall paintings of the Beni-Hassan tombs in Egypt from about 2000 BC. Nearly 1,500 years later, representations of juggling in Greek art appeared. Juggling was considered a form of recreation for the Greeks. Chinese juggling sticks are also called devil sticks as a result of the Greek term for "devil," meaning "to throw across."

After the brief history lesson, show the students examples of the kind of Chinese juggling sticks they will make during the program. Give each teen the material needed to make one:

- Two small dowels, 18" long with 3/8" diameter
- One large dowel, 24" long with 1/2" diameter
- Four rolls colored electrical tape to decorate the dowels
- Felt
- Glue
- Rolls of duct tape
- Rolls of rubber tape

Instruct the participants to wrap the colored tape in "candy cane" fashion on the large dowel. The black rubber tape will then be used to fill in the exposed wood. After rubber tape is added, participants attach felt to the ends with duct tape. The small dowels will be decorated similarly, with only two-thirds of the dowel being covered with rubber tape. Explore the Web sites in the Collection Connection for tips on using your new juggling sticks.

Collection Connection

Bulloch, Ivan and Diane James. 1997. *I Want to Be a Juggler* [photographs, Fiona Pragoff, illustrations Derek Matthews]. Chicago, IL: World Book.

Gifford, Clive. 1995. *The Usborne Book of Juggling.* London: Usborne Books.

Juggling Information Service. Available: www.juggling.org (December 2004).

Koah Fong's Juggling Page. Available: www.ntu.edu.sg/home/kfloh/juggling.htm (December 2004).

Seth and Devil Sticks. Available: www.aigeek.com/devil-stick (December 2004).

The Bottom Line

Estimate about $20.00 per program planned for 20 participants. Dowels can be ordered precut from a hardware store or hobby shop.

Teen Feedback

The teens loved them!

TEEN ART SHOW CONTEST, BY JAN CHAPMAN

Jan and her Teen Advisory Board planned a two-hour art show and contest, held in the meeting room that was transformed into an art gallery. Teens could enter artwork in the following categories: Colored Pencil Drawing, Painting, Sculpture, Pencil Drawing, Photography, and Printmaking. The deadline for submitting entries was the day prior to the art show. All entries except sculpture were required to be matted or mounted, and all entries had to be clearly labeled with the teen's name, age, and phone number on the back of the artwork.

The day before the show, volunteers from the TAB stacked boxes and draped them with black plastic tablecloths to make display stands for free-standing artwork. They used Lucite cases to display the more delicate pieces. Other artwork was hung on the walls of the meeting room. Overhead spotlights made the lighting more like an art gallery.

Jan asked four people to assist in judging. One was an art teacher from the elementary school, two were members of the community, and one a teen judge. The art was judged for the first hour of the program and then the gallery was opened to the public. Ribbons were awarded to the first-, second-, and third-place winners in each category judged. Jan had approximately 30 total entries from teen artists in the community. After the show, the winning entries were displayed in the public areas of the library for the rest of the month.

The Bottom Line

Expenses were about $25.00, which included the cost of the plastic tablecloths and the award ribbons.

Figure 4.5 A teen art show may inspire a future Van Gogh.

The Collection Connection

Display art books and how-to drawing books.

Teen Feedback

This program has run for two years now and has received very favorable comments from the teens. Jan really likes this program because it is an opportunity for teens to showcase their talents. One young lady was really thrilled to win an award and told Jan that it was the first time she had ever received any recognition for her artistic talent.

STRING ART, BY VIRGINIA SCHONWALD

The teens choose the string colors, the spacing of their nails, and a wrapping pattern, so every string-art design will be unique. You will need:

- Precut 15" square pieces of 3/4" plywood, one for each teen
- Brads with heads
- Embroidery floss in various colors
- Black spray paint

- Drawing compass
- Tack hammers

Spray paint the plywood squares and let them dry before the program. Each teen receives a wood square and draws a circle in the center, ten to twelve inches in diameter, using a compass or a large round object to trace. Mark the circle with a pencil, using a ruler to space the brads evenly. Begin hammering brads halfway into the board at opposite sides, spacing them equally around the circle.

The next step is to choose a color of embroidery floss and tie it to the nail at the top of the circle. A pattern is created by looping the string around the nails around the circle, skipping a selected number of nails evenly all the way around. For example, you could begin with green embroidery floss at the top of the circle and then skip two brads, loop it around the third and continue around the circle, looping the green floss around every third nail, going as many times around the circle as you want. Begin on another nail with a different color and repeat the process until satisfied with the design. Check out www.mathcats.com/crafts/stringart.html for patterns and design tips.

The Bottom Line

Home Depot precut and donated the plywood squares for Virginia's program. The rest of the materials cost about $20.00.

Teen Feedback

The teens enjoyed the program very much and were proud of their string-art creations.

FLIP-FLOP WORKSHOP, BY SANDY LANG

With a flip-flop workshop, teens can put their best foot forward at the library! Collect a variety of embellishments and invite teens to bring in their own flip-flops to decorate. Use hot glue guns to attach the decorations on the straps of the flip-flops. Be sure to provide decorative items in twos so teens can make matching pairs of flip-flops.

MARBLE MAGNETS, BY LARA M. ZEISES

Marble magnets have been popular with crafters for a long time. It's a quick, fun project and can be personalized as a gift. They are perfect for school lockers. To create marble magnets, you will need:

- Images—magazines, catalogs, photos, computer printouts
- 3/4" clear glass marbles with one flat side (buy more than you need, since some will come with scratches)
- 3/4" round magnets
- Glass sealer (adult supervision needed, causes skin irritation)
- Wooden craft sticks for applying glue

Collect small images, including photos and icons, from old magazines (*Entertainment Weekly* and *Blender* are great sources for small images) or have teens bring in small pictures or computer printouts from home. You could also choose to provide art supplies—small stickers, colored pens/pencils, etc.—so teens can design their own images.

Cut the images using a one-inch circle template or a one-inch craft punch. After the image has been cut or punched out, glue it to the magnet. There are two ways to do this: either purchase magnets with adhesive already on one side, or apply the glass sealer you'll use to glue the marbles to the magnets. It's a good idea to provide metal cookie sheets or Altoids tins so the participants have a place to put the magnets while the adhesive between the image and the magnet dry.

When the images are firmly affixed to the magnets after 20 to 30 minutes, apply a thin layer of glass sealer over the top of the image. Next, apply the marble (flat side down) and hold for 20 seconds or until the glass sealer starts to catch. If you are using tins, they really come in handy during this step, because you can leave the magnets in the tin and keep them there to dry. Let the magnets dry for at least six hours before actually using them.

For a gift set of marble magnets, collect a small tin for each teen to decorate to match their magnets. Six marble magnets will fit perfectly inside of a standard Altoids tin. Sand the tins with sandpaper and provide Mod Podge, tissue paper, paints, and sequins for decorating. Visit http://megan.scatterbrain.org/notmartha/tomake/marblemagnets.html to see pictures of completed sets of marble magnets.

HANG LOOSE TEEN CRAFT NIGHT, BY PHYLLIS UCHRIN

Phyllis coordinated a series of craft projects for one summer reading program. Set each craft project on a separate table. The first project is a visor teens paint with puffy fabric paint. While the visors are drying, the teens can have a snack break at another table. The next craft project is a beaded fish key ring, completed while listening to music CDs. Phyllis bought the visors and key chain kits from Oriental Trading and purchased the puffy paint at a craft store. To complete the theme, the teens were given a Hawaiian bag with a

**Figure 4.6 Posters with great graphics set
the mood and theme for a program.**

summer reading log, a magnetic picture frame that reads "aloha," a fish pencil, and a surfboard magnet, also from Oriental Trading at www.oriental
trading.com.

Figure 4.7 Leis, flowers, and tropical island crafts look like fun!

Collection Connection

Display summer reading books and recreational reading collections.

Teen Feedback

The teens said they liked having projects to work on. They filled out an evaluation form at the end of the Teen SRP. Thirty-eight percent of the teens said they attended the craft night and loved it.

FREEDOM BRICKS, BY DENISE DIPAOLO

If Paint the Library Red, White, and Blue seems like more than you want to tackle, try this creative and patriotic painting program. Freedom Bricks are painted and decoupaged bricks decorated with patriotic symbols of freedom. Denise presented this program for Martin Luther King Jr. Day, but it would work well as a summer program around Independence Day, too. Teens may choose to paint words or quotes on their bricks or decoupage symbols printed from the Internet. Squirt puddles of acrylic craft paint onto paper-plate palettes for the artists.

Some teens painted the bricks with words such as "peace," "love," "I have a dream," etc. Others chose symbols printed from the Internet: a white dove, the American flag, eagles, the Liberty Bell, a peace sign, an image of Martin Luther King Jr., etc. To use the Internet printouts, paint the brick first and then glue on the printed symbols. Some teens made a collage on their bricks, combining original painting with printouts, and others used glitter. During the project, Denise led a discussion about freedom and what it means.

After the bricks were decorated, they were sealed with Mod Podge. Each of the bricks went on display labeled with the teen's name and grade at the Library's community Martin Luther King Jr. breakfast. The bricks would look good in a display case used as bookends for the whole month.

Collection Connection

Biographies of Martin Luther King Jr. were on display for Denise's program. If the activity is used for Independence Day, American history books will look great displayed with these bricks as bookends!

The Bottom Line

The bricks were donated from a patron who had leftover bricks from a home-improvement project. Paints and other materials cost approximately $35.00.

Teen Feedback

Teens had fun painting and felt special knowing that their artwork would be on display.

FUNKADELIC 60S, BY PAULA SHOCKLEY

Tie-dye is the main attraction at this program featuring the culture of the 1960s. Begin the program outside with the tie-dye project, as it takes the most time. The teens can bring articles of clothing or pillowcases to dye. Paula's teens used dye-ties purchased from S&S Worldwide (http://www.ssww.com). They are strings that have dye in them, so there is no need for buckets of several different colors. Make sure everyone wears gloves, and follow the instructions on the package. You may want to practice using the dye-ties ahead of time. Have at least two adults help with this process.

After tying, the shirts need to be dipped into hot water to activate the dye. Paula used a baby pool filled with hot water from water urns. The teens split into groups and took turns dipping their shirts in the water until the dye was released. They then dipped the shirts in a bucket of cold water to set the dye and rinsed the shirts. When everyone finished, they removed the rubber bands from the shirts and Paula took pictures of the teens showing off their creations. The teens can play Twister, Frisbee, and hula hoops while waiting for their turns at tie-dying. Decorate with peace signs and smiley faces and play 60s music to create a funkadelic atmosphere.

The Funkadelic 60's!

Join us for groovy music, food, games and tie-dye crafts. Ages 12-17 Thursday, July 17ᵗʰ 2:00-4:00

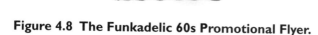

Figure 4.8 The Funkadelic 60s Promotional Flyer.

Follow the tie-dye craft with a 60s trivia game indoors. Hang a bead curtain in the doorway to the meeting room. Paula created a tic-tac-toe style board like Hollywood Squares with a different 60s clip-art icon in each of the nine squares: bell-bottoms, peace sign, yellow submarine, platform shoes, etc. Smiley faces and peace signs are the X's and O's. Gather trivia from decades in review books and trivia Web sites. Divide the teens into two teams to work together to answer the questions. The first team to get three in a row wins prizes. Offer small prizes to choose from: love beads, peace pins, tie-dyed-T-shirt-shaped notepads. The teens played the limbo at the end of the program.

The Bottom Line

Two branches held this program for a combined total of $80.00.

Teen Feedback

The teens loved the program, especially the tie-dyeing. Some of the teens who participated are VolunTeens, so they dyed their VolunTeen T-shirts, and wore them constantly. They can't wait for the 70s program the library is doing this year.

POETRY ROCKER IN YOUR LOCKER, BY JENNIFER STENCEL

Teens can create a magnetic poetry kit for their school lockers. Magnetic strips can be purchased in rolls of ten feet for about $5.00. Words can be hand written or computer printed on any paper, cut to the width of the magnetic strip, and stuck to the magnets. Use a pretty script font and colored paper for unique sets. Cut the words apart and become a poet.

SLAMMIN' IN YOUR SLEEP, BY JENNIFER STENCEL

Teens decorate their pillowcases with favorite lyrics, quotes, and poems, using Sharpie markers. This is a fun idea for a lock-in!

CARTOONING FOR TEENS, BY GRETCHEN H. HANLEY

Teens met at Gretchen's library on two Saturday afternoons for a beginning course on cartooning taught by a local cartoonist. Drawing paper and pencils selected by the cartoonist were purchased for each teen. The instructor used a drawing easel and flip chart, and the library staff checking in during the class. The second week the students brought in the work they had done during the week to build on what they had learned.

Collection Connection

Display books and videos on cartooning, manga, and anime that teens can check out.

The Bottom Line

The drawing paper was $10.00 per pad and the pencils were $1.25 each.

MANGA DRAWING CLASS, BY RHONDA BELYEA

"Learn how to draw manga. Please bring a sketchbook and a pencil. Presented by Ben Dursa, art and graphic design teacher in Baltimore, Maryland, awarded master's of art education and bachelor's of fine arts degrees from the Maryland Institute College of Art."

The first manga drawing class offered during Teen Read Week was so successful that Rhonda's library offered four more classes at four branches. For two hours, teens were taught steps and techniques for drawing characters in the popular manga style. As the teacher shows the various exercises on an overhead projector, the teens look up at the projected image and practice in the sketchbooks they bring or on the paper provided by the library.

The instructor was an experienced high school art teacher, who runs an after-school graphic design club at his high school. This program's success is dependent on the skill and experience of your instructor as both an artist and a teacher. One library staff member welcomed the teens as they arrived, mentioned the library materials available, and checked in during the program.

Collection Connection

Display manga, manga drawing books, and anime videos and DVDs.

The Bottom Line

The teacher was paid $300.00 plus expenses for mileage and lunch.

Teen Feedback

"You should have more programs like this." When asked if they'd change anything about the program, one teen said, "No way!" When asked how they'd improve upon this program, one teen said, "The only thing I'd do different is to make the program longer." (Longer than two hours, that is!) In fact, they wouldn't leave the room even after the program was over. The kids really related to the teacher and couldn't get enough of the topic. "Ben was really cool!"

BUTT PILLOWS, BY RANDEE J. BYBEE

Participants in the program need to bring an old pair of jeans. First, cut the legs off, leaving about an inch of the legs. Stitch the leg openings together with embroidery floss using an overcast stitch. Participants then choose from a variety of fabrics, trimmings, fake jewels, key chains, and other items to decorate their pillows. They can use fabric to make hearts and stars and attach them with fabric glue; to attach other items they need to use a hot glue gun.

When the pillows have been decorated and the glue is dry, stuff them with polyester fiberfill and close them up using an overcast stitch and embroidery floss. After stuffing, teens can add belts, chains, key rings, and other charms to the belt loops. Play music while everyone works on their pillows.

Along with the traditional publicity methods, Randee has a book cart that the advisory board has painted. She posts flyers on that cart and parks it at various areas around the library where teens hang out to advertise programs.

Collection Connection

Sewing, quilting, and embroidery books are on display at checkout.

Figure 4.9 Butt pillows are cool. Guys and girls enjoy making these!

The Bottom Line

Collect the decorative items from coworkers, TAB members, and friends. You can go to local fabric stores and ask for donations of items, such as needles and floss. The stuffing is the main expense.

Teen Feedback

The teens were really happy with the program. A couple went home and made more for themselves and for their siblings. Randee repeated the program and 30 teens, including eight boys, showed up!

Chapter 5

Book-themed Programs

OVERVIEW

The foundation of a library is its book collection. When we provide programming for teens at libraries, one of our main goals is to connect teens and books. One-on-one readers' advisory, book displays, booklists, face-out shelving, and book discussion groups are several of the traditional ways we do this. With a bit of creativity, you can connect teens and books with new and exciting ideas like the book-themed programs in this chapter.

BOOKS COME ALIVE, BY JANET GOOD

Some stories make such an impact that readers are left wanting more. Janet has created a program to give her volunteer teens a chance to enjoy their favorite stories and characters beyond the book. Books Come Alive combines activities, food, crafts, games, and skits for a four-hour after-hours program. The description that follows is for a program featuring *The Golden Compass* by Philip Pullman.

The Golden Compass program was made up of seven chapters or parts:

- Chapter 1: The teens act out the first chapter of the book, each one choosing a character to play. If there are more characters than teens, some can play more than one part. Try rewriting the chapter into a reader's theatre script to prompt the teens to act out their parts.
- Chapter 2: Serve Scholar's refreshments: Poppy heads are hotdog disks and wine is sparkling juice. Show pictures on an opaque projector as Lord Asriel's slide presentation. Follow the slides with a Find Your Daemon activity. Using stuffed animals, each teen chooses an animal, names it, and lists its good and bad traits.

- Chapter 3: Play Kids and Gobblers Tag. Half the teens are the kids and half are the gobblers. The kids go hide in the darkened library. The gobblers are released to go find the kids and bring them back.
- Chapter 4: Make a Golden Compass Clock from old CDs. Spray paint the CDs gold and use purchased clock workings. Print out color copies of an alethiometer from the Internet and glue to the CD to decorate the clock faces. Find a picture of the alethiometer at www.randomhouse.com/features/pullman/alethiometer. The Web site has a history and instructions for reading the alethiometer that you can print for handouts. CD clock kits can be found at www.clockparts.com/kits3.htm.
- Chapter 5: Serve Mrs. Coulter's cocktail party: canapés and punch.
- Chapters 6 and 7: Teens use the Internet computers to visit a Web site with a question-the-alethiometer activity.
- Chapters 8 and 9: Serve up a trip to the North: popsicles for a dessert and ending to the program.

Janet has also had success with a Harry Potter program created by the teen volunteers and patterned after *The Golden Compass* program. Act out two chapters, serve two refreshments sessions, have one or two craft sessions and two game sessions, pulling the ideas from the book and its characters. A future program will be based on *The Sisterhood of the Traveling Pants* by Ann Brashares. For this program, Janet plans to have four stations, each with activities and refreshments, which will represent the four places the main characters traveled to during the summer. Any favorite book can come alive with this program idea!

The Bottom Line

The main expenses for these programs are the craft materials and refreshments. Shop on the Internet, cruise craft store sale tables, ask for donations for craft materials, and make some of your own refreshments to stretch your budget. If you need a shorter two-hour version of the program, just do one skit, one craft, one game, and one refreshment break.

PYB: PROTECT YOUR BOOKS, BY CATHY HOCHADEL

"New textbooks? Ratty textbooks? Change their appearance to match your personality. All supplies provided free!"

Cathy offers this creative social program to teens after school during the first two weeks of school in the fall. Teens can cover their textbooks to protect them and make them uniquely their own. Collect leftover craft supplies around the library, from coworkers, and at home, and set them out with a good supply of Kraft paper or butcher paper. As Cathy says, "prepare to be amazed!"

Supplies to collect:

- Kraft paper, butcher paper, or fabric
- Glitter and glue
- Ribbon
- Stickers
- Decorative rubber stamps and ink pads
- Discarded popular teen magazines for pictures
- Markers
- Tape and scissors

TIME-SHARE CHAIR, BY CATHY HOCHADEL

Invite teens to read in the lap of luxury at the library! "Be spoiled and pampered while sitting in a comfortable reading chair. Sign up for your share of eight straight hours of reading. 9:00 a.m.–5:00 p.m."

Cathy begged a local furniture store for a cool chair and got a Papa San chair from Pier 1. She put down a $50.00 deposit which was returned to her when she returned the chair in good condition.

Put the chair in a place that is comfortable for reading. Teens sign up for a time and choose what they will read during their time in the chair. Have a boom box and CDs on hand so that each teen can listen to his or her favorite music with his or her own CDs and a headset. As soon as the teen arrives for his or her time-share, take him or her to the chair. When s/he is comfortably seated, offer food and drink and position the boom box so it is easily accessible. The morning shifts get juice and granola bars. The lunch shifts get cheese, grapes, crackers, and juice, and the afternoon shifts get cookies, Tootsie Pops, and soft drinks. Be sure to have some fabric spot remover available, just in case! Ten minutes before the teen's time is up, let him/her know that another teen will be taking over the chair. Allow a few minutes between participants to brush out crumbs and check for any food or drink to be cleaned up.

TEEN ANIME CLUB, BY SHANNAN SWORD

YALSA's Teen Read Week theme "Get Graphic @ Your Library" triggered requests for more programs about graphic novels and comics at Shannan's library. Teens who love anime and manga enjoy a club that meets regularly to share their hobby. Anime and manga are the popular Japanese forms of animation in print and film.

Shannan's Teen Anime Club meets every other Saturday from 2:00 to 4:00 p.m. during the school year and once a week on a weekday during the summer from 2:00 to 4:00 p.m. Posters, newsletter articles, and word of mouth publicize the club.

These enthusiastic teens usually arrive at the library early on meeting days to peruse the shelves for new manga and anime, and some members also maintain their own Web sites. The meetings are flexible enough to accommodate several activities. The teens enjoy showing their Web site updates to their fellow club members and sharing their own new anime acquisitions. They may play *Yu-Gi-Oh* card duels, draw anime and manga, and work on stories while discussing their shared interests.

Due to their interest in games other than *Yu-Gi-Oh*, Shannan started a teen gaming club that also meets weekly. They enjoy role-playing games, board games, and other card games. Teens enjoy clubs because they can meet others who share their interests.

Collection Connection

Share new manga and anime books, magazines, and films with this appreciative group. Shannan suggests the magazines *Animerica* and *Shonen Jump*. How-to-draw-anime books would also be of interest. A book club that focuses on one area of the YA collection can be helpful to you as you work on collection development. The club members will make excellent recommendations for purchases.

The Bottom Line

Even though this is an ongoing program that meets weekly, the costs are very low. Supply paper and pencils for drawing. Members can bring their own snacks or they can eat leftover snacks from other programs. Only one staff member is needed to supervise the group.

Teen Feedback

From Shannan: I have been regularly informed about how "cool" I am for having this program. Teens are very pleased (and have said so) that I show interest in learning about their interest in anime/manga and love that "unlike some other adults I don't make them feel stupid, or like a freak for loving this stuff." I have been granted the title of "Shannan-sama" (from a Japanese term of respect). My favorite quote from this group: "Shannan-sama, you're the coolest adult we know." Why? Well, everyone likes to be seen as "cool" in the eyes of their patrons for things they've done. But aside from being "accepted" into their group in a way, they still recognize and respect me as an adult role model. Recently when one of the members of the group arrived early for a game club meeting she asked me what I was working on. I explained to her that I was working on a presentation I was giving to a group at the high school the next day about "Asset Development." When I explained the concept of assets helping teens make wise decisions about drugs and other destructive activities and the importance of positive adult role models, she pointed excitedly at me and said "Like you!" I'm grinning again now as I write this because of how great it made me feel.

BATTLE OF THE BOOKS, BY AMY HOPTAY

April marks the annual Battle of the Books, one-and-a-half-hour events held in the high school auditorium and coordinated by Amy's library. The middle school competes on one night, the high school on another. Publicity begins in January; a news release goes to the local paper, the library newsletter, and the school papers. Flyers for every student are sent out to the schools with registration forms for teams. Each team needs no fewer than four and no more than five teen members and an adult to act as team manager.

Keep a checklist throughout the year of book titles to use for the program and order multiple paperback copies of each title in January. In early February hold an organizational meeting at the library to distribute the lists of books for each Battle. The school librarians have been known to leak the titles, giving some kids an unfair advantage, so it is a top-secret list until this meeting! At the meeting you will meet the teams, go over the rules of the Battle, explain how the competition works, state the manager's responsibilities, etc.

At the competition the teams are seated on the stage. The team managers switch seats so they are scoring for a team other than their own. Every round is composed of one question from each book. The teams each choose a scribe who writes their answers on a pad and a team manager who answers the question for the team. Each group has 20 seconds to agree on an answer to a question. The scribe then tears off the answer paper, gives it to the team manager, and each team manager reads the answer. One team answers the first question first, another team the second question first, etc. The answers are scored as follows: one point is awarded for the author's name and four points for the correct answer to the question, for a total of five points per question. If a group only gets the author correct, they earn one point; if the group only answers the question, they get four points. The team with the most points at the end of two rounds (sometimes three, depending on the number of teams) is the winner.

In 2004, Amy had 15 middle school teams and ten high school teams. There were 14 titles on the middle school list and 12 on the high school list. On the night of the Battle, staff members and volunteer librarians from the schools helped with the program: you will need a timekeeper, three judges, and a microphone person who goes from group to group to let each team give its answer to a question. Other librarians at the library and at the school read one or two titles from the list and help write the questions for the Battle. Those same people should attend the competition, in case there is a debate over an answer! You might wish to set up times for book discussions in the weeks following the Battle so the students can come and talk about all the books they read.

Collection Connection

Choose book titles from the teen department and purchase multiple copies (at least five) in paperback. Titles that form part of a series may encourage the teens to keep reading.

The Bottom Line

Amy's library pays for five paperback copies of each title, and borrows more copies from other libraries. Prizes are donated from local businesses for the winners. Everyone involved gets some kind of participation prize. A local bookstore donates $0.50 off a paperback to everyone, a first prize of $10 per person for the winning team, and $5 per person for the second place team. In addition, there is a consortium of school and public librarians that donates money for additional incentives for the high school teams. Partnering with schools and soliciting businesses for donations are wise steps when putting together a large program, not only for financial help, but also for help with the publicity and implementation of the program.

Teen Feedback

One of the most interesting parts of the Battle is finding out which books the teens liked most and least. This can be done while the judges are tallying scores.

FOLKTALES, BY MELISSA PILLOT

Middle school students explore folktales in this one-hour after-school program. Melissa begins her program by telling her audience about folktales and trickster tales and follows with the telephone game to show how a story can change in five minutes, not to mention 500 years! To play the telephone game, whisper a short story—just a few sentences—to one teen. The teens then pass the story around the room, one by one, whispering each time. The last person who hears the story tells it aloud to the group and you tell the original version to compare the two versions. Follow the game by reading a folktale to the audience.

The rest of the program is performed by the teens. Display short printed folktales and folktale books and give the teens time to look them over to choose tales they would like to read. You will need cassette recorders, blank audio tapes, labels for the cassettes, and pens. When the teens read aloud to the group, record their stories on audio cassettes and allow them to listen to their own voices if they would like to. Label each cassette with the teen presenter's name and the title of the folktale. The teens take home the cassettes to share with family and friends.

Collection Connection

Folktale titles for this program included:

Brown, David K. "Folklore, Myth, and Legend." Available: www.ucalgary.ca/ ~dkbrown/storfolk.html (December 2004).

Chowdhury, Rohini. "Long, Long Time Ago: Stories for Children." Available: www.longlongtimeago.com (December 2004).

DeSpain, Pleasant. 2001. *Tales of Tricksters.* Illustrations by Don Bell. Little Rock, AR: August House.

Hamilton, Virginia. 1993. *The People Could Fly: American Black Folktales.* New York: Knopf Books for Young Readers; Reprint edition (January 4).

Law, Alice. 1994. *Spooky Stories for a Dark & Stormy Night.* Illustrated by Gahan Wilson. 1st ed. New York: Hyperion Books for Children.

Lindy, Elaine L. "Absolutely Whootie: Stories to Grow By." Available: www.storiestogrowby.com (December 2004).

McDermott, Gerald. 1997. *Arrow to the Sun: A Pueblo Indian Tale.* Harmondsworth [Eng.]: Kestrel Books.

Molnar, Irma. 2001. *One-Time Dog Market at Buda and other Hungarian Folktales.* Illustrations by Georgeta-Elena Ene, sel. North Haven, CT: Linnet Books.

Schlosser, Sandra E. "American Folklore." Available: www.americanfolklore.net (December 2004).

The Bottom Line

The ten handheld cassette players, left over from another program, had cost about $20.00 a piece. Cassettes were purchased in bulk and cost about $0.15 a piece.

Teen Feedback

The teens loved recording themselves and playing the story over and over again!

BANNED BOOKS, BY DEBBIE SOCHA

High school students will enjoy a good heated discussion about censorship in a program featuring Banned Books. Contact English teachers and suggest to them they might encourage attendance at this program by offering extra credit. Mention free pizza in the publicity to pull in more teens! Debbie had 50 teens come to this program and suggests that three staff members be present.

Begin by explaining what "banned" and "challenged" means, and allow the teens to express whether they feel it is ever appropriate to ban a book, and if so, when. Continue the discussion by talking about what types of materials might be challenged. Useful resources include www.ala.org, http://onlinebooks.library.upenn.edu/banned-books.html, and discussion material included in the Novelist database.

Break up the audience into groups of three to five students. Give each group several challenged books to look at, and ask them to try to decide why they were challenged. Include juvenile, young adult, and adult books. Each group then reports which books they discussed and why they think they were challenged. The teens may also want to discuss books assigned in their schools that have been challenged by parents.

Wrap about a dozen challenged or banned books in brown paper. Write on the front of each a short description of its content. Teens can guess the titles of the books for a prize. Serve pizza and soda while the teens are working independently on this activity.

Collection Connection

Display challenged books that can be checked out. Include any titles that have been challenged in your own library.

The Bottom Line

Soda and pizza are the main expenses. A gift certificate to a book store is a perfect prize for the independent wrapped-book quiz.

Teen Feedback

Teens really enjoyed the program; many of them thanked Debbie for doing it. The high school teacher who most heavily promoted it e-mailed Debbie to tell her that she heard positive feedback from her students and that they continued the discussion in some of her classes.

BOOKS-ON-TAPE CLUB, BY MARK A. MALCOLM

The Books-on-tape Club is a collaboration between a middle school and the Maynard Public Library. About a dozen middle school students get together on Thursdays after school for six weeks to record early chapter books on tape for elementary-aged kids. Each student reads a different chapter of the book. The book and the tape is put together into a kit and circulated in the library.

Blank tapes, a recorder with a microphone, and snacks for the teens are all you need. One staff member and one volunteer can coordinate the program. Suggested series are *Marvin Redpost, Magic Tree House, Junie B. Jones,* and *The Bailey School Kids.*

Teen Feedback

The kits are going like hotcakes! The teens feel like real big shots because their voices are being heard in the cars of people all over town. "We're all going to be famous." "It's hard to read with pretzels in your mouth." "I didn't think I'd have this much fun reading out loud."

ALL-YOU-CAN-READ BUFFET, BY KARA FALCK

Saturday of Teen Read Week is a great time to hold an All-you-can-read Buffet. From 11:30 a.m. to 7 p.m., teens are served up great reads and great food for a day that fills your mind and stomach! Begin registration on October 1 so you can plan for the number of participants.

When teens check in between 11:30 and 11:45 a.m. on the day of the buffet, give them a name tag and a menu. The menu includes the itinerary for the day, food and beverage choices, book choices, and the rules of the program. The books are divided into appetizers, main course, and desserts on the menu. Display the books and magazines on a table set with a tablecloth, place settings, serving bowls, candles, and a centerpiece. After check-in, the teens choose a reading spot and settle in. At 11:50, go over the rules and so everyone can start reading at 12 noon. Teens can bring bean bag chairs, a pillow, or a sleeping bag for comfort and stake their claim on their spot for the day.

The Teen Advisory Board helped make the rules for Kara's buffet:

- Read the entire time silently.
- Read anything.
- No books on tape or CD.
- No Walkmans.
- No computers.
- No doodling or writing.

The readers get five-minute breaks every hour to get food, go to the restroom, get more books, and stretch. If a teen breaks one rule, he receives a warning. If he gets two warnings, he is disqualified.

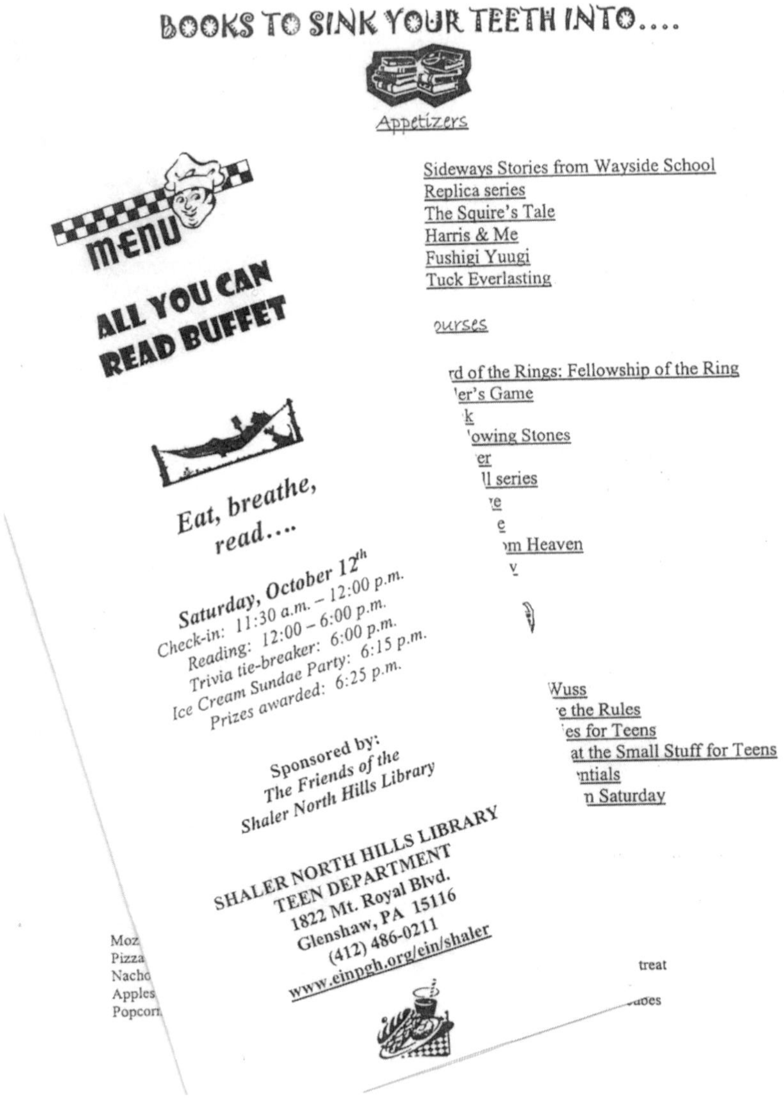

BOOKS TO SINK YOUR TEETH INTO....

Appetizers

Sideways Stories from Wayside School
Replica series
The Squire's Tale
Harris & Me
Fushigi Yuugi
Tuck Everlasting

MENU

ALL YOU CAN
READ BUFFET

ourses

rd of the Rings: Fellowship of the Ring
'er's Game
k
'owing Stones
er
ll series
'e
e
m Heaven
v

Eat, breathe,
read....

Saturday, October 12th
Check-in: 11:30 a.m. – 12:00 p.m.
Reading: 12:00 – 6:00 p.m.
Trivia tie-breaker: 6:00 p.m.
Ice Cream Sundae Party: 6:15 p.m.
Prizes awarded: 6:25 p.m.

Wuss
'e the Rules
es for Teens
at the Small Stuff for Teens
'ntials
n Saturday

Sponsored by:
The Friends of the
Shaler North Hills Library

SHALER NORTH HILLS LIBRARY
TEEN DEPARTMENT
1822 Mt. Royal Blvd.
Glenshaw, PA 15116
(412) 486-0211
www.einpgh.org/ein/shaler

Moz
Pizza
Nacho   treat
Apples
Popcorn   .aoes

**Figure 5.1 A menu serves as a program for the All-you-can-read
Buffet, suggesting titles for each meal course.**

The food buffet can include chips, veggies and dip, apples and dip, cheese
and Triscuits, tortilla chips and nacho dip, granola bars, Swedish fish, cookies, brownies, pizza rolls, cheese sticks, mozzarella sticks, bookworm Rice
Crispy treats, and bagel bites. Borrow toaster ovens from home to prepare
the hot foods. To keep food preparation and serving simpler, just serve hot

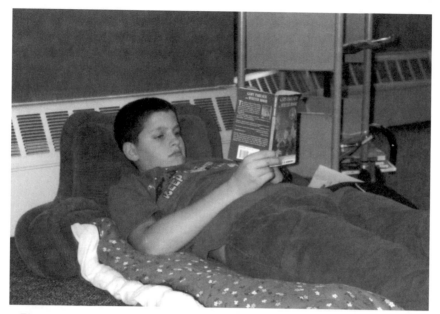

Figure 5.2 This teen reader enjoys books and yummy snacks while settled in at the library for the day.

foods for a two-hour period in the afternoon and save desserts for late in the afternoon. TAB members can bring additional snacks to share. Request all participants to bring a two liter beverage to help cut costs. The food is served by helpers when a reader raises a hand to order from the menu. The server also brings books and magazines as requested.

Six volunteers are suggested—three to watch kids reading and get books, and three to handle food. Whisper to announce break time to set the tone. Two groups can take a break at the top of the hour, and two groups at the bottom of the hour to minimize noise and commotion. Teens can quit reading at any time, but are out of the competition if they do.

Announce the end at 6 p.m. Distribute answer sheets to all remaining teens for a tie-breaker quiz of 15 trivia questions. The questions can include book quotes, general definitions, word unscrambles, and questions about the library. Ask the helpers to grade the quizzes while you go over the answers with the teens. Close the event with an ice-cream sundae bar.

Collection Connection

The menu of books can be supplemented with any reading lists or booklists that you have available. See the menu for the titles suggested for this event.

The Bottom Line

The Friends of the Library provided the funds for food and prizes for Kara's program. The TAB contributed snacks, the staff donated baked goods, and each participant brought a two-liter drink. The first-place winner received a $50.00 gift certificate to a local mall, second place received $15.00, and third place received $10.00. Everyone received a key chain and pixie sticks.

FREE COMIC BOOK DAY, BY TINA GENTILE

Comics and graphic novels have rightfully found their places in young adult library collections. Particularly attractive to boys and reluctant readers, many graphic novels and comics have beautiful and exciting artwork. YALSA's Teen Read Week theme "Get Graphic @ Your Library" brought these collections into the limelight and many libraries presented programs to promote the collections. Libraries are also participating in Free Comic Book Day, an annual nationwide event. See www.freecomicbookday.com for details about receiving your free comics to give away.

Tina's library made the most of Free Comic Book Day by adding program activities to the day. To reproduce her successful program, play a video of Stan Lee or another available artist, offer Superman ice cream and a Spiderman cake for refreshments, and invite an artist to give instruction on drawing comic-book characters. Give all participants one or two free comic books available from your local comics shop. Most shops will also have buttons, bookmarks, posters, and window clings for additional prizes or giveaways.

To promote Free Comic Book Day and your collection, order the DC Universe poster and bookmarks from the ALA store at www.alastore.ala.org. For a real challenge, number all the characters on the poster and hang it in the YA room. Create numbered answer sheets for teens to identify all the characters on the poster.

Collection Connection

Display graphic novels, comics, how-to-draw-books, and comics related videos. A bibliography of available materials will encourage teens to place holds on titles that are in branches or checked out.

The Bottom Line

The comics are free unless you request a lot of them for many branches from one store, in which case there may be a small charge. Additional activities can be added, depending upon your budget.

READ-A-THON, BY PHYLLIS UCHRIN

An evening of reading, snacks, and games for prizes celebrated Teen Read week at Phyllis's library. A Read-a-thon can also be scheduled as part of a lock-in or on a Saturday. Teachers may be interested in offering extra credit for this reading program. Contact them in advance of the program, provide bookmarks with the program information to pass out to their students, and inform the teachers which students attended after the program is over.

A thermometer chart is a good visual to show how much reading they are accomplishing through the program. Draw a thermometer shape on a poster, mark off 15-minute segments; color in one segment for every 15 minutes each teen has read throughout the program. Try a series of read-a-thons in the summer and reward the teens with a visit to a swimming pool when the thermometer shows them to be hot readers!

A sample schedule for the Read-a-thon program follows:

- Introductions and announcements
- Reading time
- Pizza and snack time
- Reading time
- READO game (create a library bingo game)
- Reading time
- Famous First Lines quiz. Available: http://quiz.ivillage.com/readersandwriters/tests/firstlines.htm
- Reading time
- READO
- Giveaways: books for everyone and winners of games

Collection Connection

Display popular new titles, popular series, and new collections.

The Bottom Line

Ask your Friends group for funds to purchase current titles in paperback for prizes. Collect free books when possible from conferences and publishers and save them for prizes.

Teen Feedback

"When will we do this again?" The school media specialist told Phyllis about three boys who came to her the day after the event and told her how cool the library is and how much fun they had at the Read-a-thon!

Celebrate Teen Read Week at the
Dunedin Public Library.

Join us Monday, October 20, 2003 for a
TEEN READ-A-THON

5:00 – 8:00PM

Youth Program Room

Stop in and see how long you can read.
Games, prizes and food!

Ages 12-18
Registration Required

For more information, contact Youth Services at 298-3080 x240

Figure 5.3 The publicity flyer for the Read-a-thon.

TOTAL READING LIVE, BY CARLY WIGGINS

Teens enjoy discussing current topics and learn about searching electronic databases for periodicals at this monthly half-hour after-school program. Mail postcards to young adults who participate in other programs and distribute posters and flyers to promote the program. Choose an article from a maga-

Figure 5.4 The teens show off their accomplishment on a poster of a thermometer. The temperature rose with each 15 minutes of reading.

zine that will appeal to teens for the first session. Suggested topics that have worked well are:

- Should the *Harry Potter* books be banned?
- Are cigarettes being marketed to teens?

Articles written by teens for teens are preferable. After the first session, the teens can choose the future topics for discussion.

Make copies of the article for each participant. The article can be read aloud round-robin style. Allow discussion of the ideas in the article for about 20 to 30 minutes. Increase information literacy by sharing the source of the article, how and where it was found, the background of the author, why the article was written, and any other information that is available in the database.

This program can be altered to meet the needs and interests of the young adults in the group. For example, Carly's teens are fans of a local band. One month they read an article about the band, and she invited the band's vocalist to come to the discussion. The young adults were surprised and delighted, and were able to ask him questions based on what they had read.

Collection Connection

Select the articles from the electronic databases available in your library, and highlight those during the discussion. Show teens how to search for more articles about the topic in the database.

The Bottom Line

Photocopying or printing the articles is the only necessary expense. Snacks can be provided if funds are available. Always check with other departments of the library for leftover snacks that can be frozen or saved for your programs!

CAFÉ BOOK, BY REBECCA PURDY

Café Book meets one day a week on a biweekly basis at the local middle schools from October through May. The 20–35 minute book discussion sessions are held during school lunch periods.

The school librarians visit each English class to promote the program. The participating school and public librarians meet with selected Café Book graduates to choose young adult titles from the current publishing year to booktalk. One public library staff member works with each school librarian.

The school and public librarians booktalk the selected titles, and a book discussion among the students follows at the meetings. A pizza party is held in May and teens vote for their Top Teen Picks from the introduced titles. The public library creates and distributes the booklists for the Top Teen Picks from each school and posts the lists on the library's Web page, www.teens point.org. In June, the students come to the public library to hear a guest speaker and vote for the Ultimate Top Teen Picks list.

Duplicate copies of the chosen titles on the lists are needed to ensure that the students are able to read the books their fellow participants and library mentors have gotten them excited about. The public library supplies three copies and the school adds two more.

Collection Connection

The entire program is based on books in both the school and public library collections. Extra copies of the selected titles are bought by both entities and circulated through the school library to participants.

The Bottom Line

Expenses included books, staff time, publicity, bookmark printing, pizza, speakers' fees, and hotel expenses. Funding comes from a combination of library budget and Friends money.

Teen Feedback

In the end-of-the-year surveys, the teens were asked "What best expresses your feelings about Café Book?" Fifty-eight participants said it was the perfect mix of reading for fun and school, 50 just loved it! What did participants like best? (They were allowed to choose more than one response.) One hundred and eleven said the pizza party, 90 said hearing about great books, 72 said the end-of-the-year Get Together Day at the public library, and 70 liked voting for titles for the bookmark. What should stay the same in future Café Book programs? Fifty-nine said everything! And 35 said the pizza!

Chapter 6

Food Programs

OVERVIEW

How many times have you heard YA librarians say "If you feed them, they will come?" There is no doubt about it, teens need to eat and a snack is part of a lot of our programming. Why not go "whole hog" and make food the main ingredient of a fun program at the library? Be sure to ask for donations for these food programs to cut expenses.

FEAR FACTOR, BY LINDA UHLER

Linda's library partnered with a local restaurant to challenge teens to eat food that was not too appealing. There were two rounds to the competition and the contestants were timed as they went through the stations. The three contestants with the shortest total times were awarded first-, second-, and third-place certificates and custom-made T-shirts that say, "I survived Teen Fear Factor 2003 @ Holmes County District Public Library." The partnering restaurant's logo is printed on the sleeve of the shirt.

For Fear Factor, you will need food, plastic cups, small paper plates, and bottled water for the participants. Linda recommends providing two lined garbage cans labeled "Barf Buckets," just in case! The parents sign permission slips for their teens to participate. The food stations are set up on two 8' tables. The contestants ring a bell to signal the end of their round, and their time is recorded. Linda's timekeeper was a TAB member who also announced the contestant's time. Another TAB member checked the contestants' mouths after each round to be sure the food was swallowed.

The Bottom Line

The cost of this program was $80.00.

The Fear Factor Stations		
Round 1	Station 1	6 oz banana pepper rings
	Station 2	4 oz Spam
	Station 3	1 purple pickled egg
	Station 4	6 oz prune juice
Round 2	Station 5	4 oz Brussels sprouts
	Station 6	4 oz sardines in mustard sauce
	Station 7	4 oz chicken livers
	Station 8	6 oz tonic water

Figure 6.1 The food challenges were arranged in stations.

Figure 6.2 A newsletter ad promoting the Fear Factor program.

Fear Factor Recipes by Jan Chapman

Barf Dip
1 cup of softened cream cheese
1 small can of cream corn
1/2 can of kraut juice
Mix the ingredients. Then drizzle a little juice from the canned corn into the mixture. Serve with tortilla chips.

Cat Puke Casserole
1 large can of Vienna sausages cut in half
1 can cream of mushroom soup
1/4 cup of ketchup
1/4 cup of pickle relish
Mix ingredients just enough to swirl them together for that "puke" effect.

Maggots in Green Sauce
Mix one can of La Choy bean sprouts with 1 small jar of green vegetable baby food. Mix well. Just tell the participants that the maggots were refrigerated which explains the lack of movement.

Green Snot Shake
In a blender, mix one package frozen chopped spinach, 1 cup of vanilla ice cream, 1/4 cup of kraut juice. Blend and serve.

Bloody Mess Dessert
1 can of anchovies
1/2 bag of frozen whole strawberries
Arrange the anchovies on a platter with the whole strawberries. Pour the remaining strawberry juice over the plate and serve.

**Figure 6.3 A few less-than-appetizing recipes
to try at your Fear Factor program.**

Teen Feedback

The teens loved this program and the winners wear their T-shirts a lot!

MAKE-IT–TAKE-IT EDIBLE VALENTINE TREATS
FOR TEENS, BY THERESA WORDELMANN

On the Wednesday evening before Valentine's Day, teens can come to the library to decorate heart-shaped cookies. You will need to bake the heart-shaped cookies the day before, making the dough from scratch or using a cookie mix when it is on sale. You will also need to buy candy toppings: miniature M&Ms, cinnamon red hots, and conversation hearts. Right before the program, make royal icing. Provide wax paper, paper towels, and paper plates. It's helpful to have a volunteer who knows how to decorate cookies help you bake the cookies and assist at the program. If you do not know someone personally, local craft stores or bakeries might be able to recommend someone. If you have the budget, you can order undecorated heart-shaped cookies from a bakery.

Set up tables in a giant square so that all program participants can sit together. Cover the tables with plastic cloths as the icing does get a little messy. Set up a supplies table at the front of the room. This table will hold all undecorated cookies, toppings, icing, paper plates, and paper towels. Place the toppings in bowls.

As the teens enter the room, the volunteer prepares individual wax-paper icing bags for each participant. Tell the teens about the supplies that are available, give them tips on using an icing bag, and remind them to be quick about placing toppings because the icing sets up quickly. The teens introduce themselves to each other and then form a line at the supply table. They choose one cookie, one bag of icing, and an assortment of toppings. After they complete their first cookie, they are invited to take a second. The program will last about one hour and 15 minutes.

For handouts, photocopy recipes for the sugar cookies and royal icing, and type out tips on making wax-paper icing bags. You can also include information about local craft stores where they can purchase disposable plastic icing bags. This program can be repeated at Christmas time with tree cut-out cookies.

Collection Connection

Theresa booktalked recent reads she thought were great during the program.

The Bottom Line

The program generally costs between $25.00 and $30.00, depending on the number of teens who sign up. Try to provide at least two cookies per teen.

Teen Feedback

This is my second year coming to the Valentine's Day Make-it–Take-it and once again the cookies were great and loads of fun. It's a great event to do! Meghan Byrnes, 9th grade

The Valentine's Day Cookie program was really a lot of fun. It really helped me get to know people I wouldn't normally be with, while doing my favorite thing: eating. I normally wouldn't have hung out at the Library, but now I'm sure I will be here more often. Jessica Kelly, 11th grade

This Valentine's Day Cookie Decorating was so much fun. I had a great time decorating a cookie with my best friend! Jennifer Conticchio, 11th grade

This program is great because it brought so many different people together to have a great Valentine's Day with each other. Suboohi Khan, 12th grade

This program was a lot of fun and very unique! Shyam Gusani, 8th grade

This program was a lot of fun. It's a great way to express yourself in an edible and decorative way. Katie Meyer, 7th grade

It was extra fantastic. It was, quite simply, fantabulous! It was, quite simply, the most wonderful thing I have ever seen. And, it is thanks to the cookies. Brian Carrasquilla, 8th grade

TEEN BAKE-OFF, BY MARGIE WALKER

A two-hour Teen Bake-off was part of Margie Walker's library's Summer Reading Program. Teens signed up before the bake-off and told Margie what they were going to make. The night of the event the 16 participants brought their gourmet baked goods. Each entry had a card with the name of the dessert in front of it. Judges from three local restaurants tasted all of the entries and decided which three were the best. The judges took their job very seriously and made the difficult decision of picking the best. The winners received $20.00 gift certificates to the judges' restaurants. Margie provided paper plates, napkins, soda, cups, forks, and spoons. Eleven girls and five boys competed, and 55 people watched the event and got a chance to taste the desserts when the competition was over.

Collection Connection

Display cookbooks for young adults and specialty cookbooks featuring brand-name ingredients that teens would like.

The Bottom Line

The judges provided the prizes and the Friends of the Amesbury Public Library funded the supplies.

Teen Feedback

Margie heard the teens say "it was really cool."

Figure 6.4 Teen Bake-off promotional poster.

Figure 6.5 Teens wait nervously nearby while a judge records her opinions of their creations.

SUNDAE, SUNDAE, BY RIA NEWHOUSE

Teens at Ria's library created their county's longest ice-cream sundae! As part of the Summer Reading Program, the event was a great way to cool down and fill bellies. Ria bought four plastic rain gutters from Home Depot and lined them up diagonally across the meeting room on painting tarps. Be sure to wash the rain gutters or line them with foil. You will need several ice-cream scoopers, lots of paper towels and plenty of freezer space. Ria bought all the toppings you can imagine—strawberry, butterscotch, caramel, whipped cream, nuts, candy, bananas, sprinkles, and candy shell. Five gallons of ice cream and about $75.00 worth of toppings later, teens were lined up at the trough enjoying a forty-foot sundae. The town newspaper came and took some great photos that appeared in the paper.

The Bottom Line

The entire program cost about $100.00. The rain gutter costs about $3.00 for ten feet. Plastic tarps are less than $1.00 each.

Figure 6.6 Teens enjoy a 40' sundae treat they made themselves.

CELEBRATE OHIO MAKING BUCKEYES, BY JANET ONEACRE

Buckeyes, yummy candies that are easy and fun to make, are famous in Ohio. The recipe is simple and the project can be neatly divided to fit the time you have and the age of the children or teens who will participate. Janice made the peanut-butter mixture ahead of time for her middle school teens. The teens then rolled the mixture into balls and dipped them into the melted chocolate. After the chocolate hardens, the buckeyes can be taken home in ziplock bags. A discussion of Ohio authors and the Ohio State Buckeyes completed the program. Older teens can take the project from start to finish at a lock-in or after-hours party where you have other activities to do while the peanut-butter mixture chills.

Buckeyes Recipe

24 ounces confectioners' sugar
16 ounces crunchy peanut butter
1 cup butter or margarine, softened

Mix butter and peanut butter together thoroughly. Add confectioners' sugar and mix well. Shape into 1-inch balls; place on wax paper lined cookie sheet and refrigerate one hour or until firm.

12 ounces semisweet chocolate chips
1 tablespoon shortening

Melt chocolate chips and shortening together in a double boiler or microwave. balls with toothpick and dip ball into the chocolate to cover most of it. Place chocolate side down on cookie sheet, smoothing over or filling in toothpick gaps with more chocolate, if necessary. Refrigerate buckeyes for about 15 minutes longer, or until the chocolate is set.

Store buckeyes tightly covered in refrigerator.

Makes about 5 dozen buckeyes candies.

**Figure 6.7 Buckeyes are a seasonal Ohio
treat that are good wherever you live.**

Chapter 7

More Parties, Games, and Lock-ins

OVERVIEW

Teens want to be with their friends. They rush home from school to get on the phone or the computer to message each other about the day's events and decide where they are going to hang out for the evening. Later they rush home from hanging out to get on the phone and computer to talk about the evening's events and to plan tomorrow's! Teens need positive social interaction and a place to be safe and comfortable together and to express themselves. The library is a wonderful place for teens to gather if there is a welcoming atmosphere and a place designed to accommodate their normal social behaviors. They want to talk and be active and creative after a long day of classroom atmosphere. They also want to eat!

Parties, games, and lock-ins are collected together in this chapter because they all require many of the same elements: space, food, extra staff, and planned activities. Lock-ins are extended parties that may include a wide variety of activities, from some of the craft projects in Chapter 3, book programs in Chapter 4, to games and movies. Lock-ins can be read-a-thons held during the day or night, an after-hours party, or an all-night slumber party. Provide interesting and fun parties, games, and lock-ins like the ones in this chapter to make your library a community center teens will want to visit.

TEEN GAME NIGHT, BY PHYLLIS UCHRIN

Teens are invited to the library every Thursday evening all summer long for a game and snack program. In a community or meeting room where teens can talk and eat, set out board and card games on tables. UNO, Cranium, and Taboo are some teen favorites. You might like to try an ice-breaker game if you have teens from several different schools so they can get to know each

Teen Game Night
Thursday, July 10, 2003
6:00 - 8:00 PM

Join us for an evening of games, pizza and fun!

Test out your Trivia Pursuit knowledge, have a
group that is unstoppable in Taboo, or just play
some board games you loved as a kid.

Pre-registration required.
Registration begins June 23, 2003.
For those in grades 6-12.

Figure 7.1 The Teen Game Night promotional poster.

other. Phyllis starts out the game night by dividing the teens into two groups to play Taboo, after which they break for pizza, snacks, and cookies. The teens then play the individual board games for 45 minutes, play a ring-toss game together, and then go back to the board games. The winners receive books as prizes.

**Figure 7.2 Games and food are all teens need
for a good time at the library.**

Collection Connection

Display game books, chess puzzle books, and look-and-find books. YA fiction books are given as prizes.

The Bottom Line

Phyllis spent $100.00 on games that can be used over and over. Patrons may donate games and teens can bring favorites to help the budget go further.

DOPPELGANGER, BY CATHY HOCHADEL

The word "Doppelganger" is the name given to a person's ghostly double. In this game, teens will try to match answers with one of their friends (the Doppelganger) to score points. There is no limit to the number of teens who can play, and it is a great game for lock-ins and Halloween parties.

You will need name tags for the players, name cards for selecting the Doppelganger, game pads and pencils or whiteboards and markers for each player, game questions (see Figure 7–3), a Questions Box for questions, a Players' Box for name cards, a stopwatch, and a score sheet. Write all the players' names down the left side of a sheet of paper for the score sheet and place a hash mark by the name each time a player gets a point. Type the game questions on scrap paper, cut them apart, and put them in the Questions Box. Write the players' names on cards and put them in the Players' Box.

Right before the program, arrange a staggered row of chairs (to prevent cheating) facing two chairs, one for the emcee and one for the Doppelganger.

The librarian explains the way the game is played, and becomes the emcee for the first game. It is extremely important to emphasize that players should write the first response that comes to mind—not to try to come up with the best answer, because the goal is to match answers with the Doppelganger.

From the Players Box, the emcee first draws a name card; the person whose name is drawn is the Doppelganger for the first game. The emcee discards the player's name card, and the Doppelganger sits in the Doppelganger's chair. The emcee draws a question from the Questions Box. The emcee reads the question aloud, beginning with the statement, "On your Game Pad, write . . ." and then repeats the question one time; he or she then starts the time clock for ten seconds. Each contestant writes his or her answer on the Game Pad, but does not allow anyone else to see what's written; and the Doppelganger writes his/her answer on the Game Pad, but does not reveal his/her answer either. After ten seconds, the emcee calls time and all writing must stop. One by one, the contestants must show their answers, even if their game pad is blank or their answer is incomplete. Then the Doppelganger's answer is revealed. One point is awarded to each contestant whose answer matches *exactly* that of the Doppelganger's. A point can be awarded for partial answers, if it is obvious that the answers would have matched. Allowances should also be made for misspellings. If there is a dispute, the decision to allow or disallow the point will be made by the emcee. Play continues through ten questions.

The person who has the most matches with the Doppelganger is the winner of that game and becomes the emcee for the next game. In the event of a tie, the winner can be determined by a coin toss. The new emcee draws a name from the Players Box, and that person then becomes the Doppelganger; the previous Doppelganger becomes a contestant.

A LIBRARY LOCK-IN,
BY KARISSA MURPHY AND ANDREA SCHIMPF

Karissa and Andrea host two lock-ins per year that attract a large number of teens, so they limit the crowd to 50. The group gathers in the community room for instructions and the rules of the evening. Then they all carpool to the local movie theatre for a midnight showing of a new movie on the opening day. They choose a movie based on a Harry Potter book or *Lord of the Rings*. After the movie they carpool back to the library and settle in for the rest of the evening.

Parents sign permission slips for the teens. The rules for the night are:

Sample Doppelganger Questions

On your pad, write…
a well-known Halloween symbol
the name of a Rock N Roll band
the name of a Hollywood couple.
a kind of bird
a color that eyes can be
a cool car
a common last name
a love song from the 90's
the name of one of the 7 dwarfs
a title for a relative (e.g. aunt)
a brass musical instrument
a fruit flavored candy
the names of a famous pair of siblings
a grade in middle school
a Biblical disciple
something you find in downtown Dayton
a hair color
the age you can start to date
a book you read in elementary school
a kind of hand tool
the best TV show on Saturday night (S,M,T,W,Th,F)
a football team
a college in the Greater Dayton area
a kind of airplane
a city or town that borders Dayton
a board game that only two people can play
a circus animal
the name of a famous dog
the name of one of Santa's reindeer
a favorite kind of sandwich
a movie playing at the theatres today
a name for a black cat
the name of something you find in a bathroom cabinet
a TV witch
a flavor of Kool-Aid
a professional extreme sport athlete
a typical weight of a bowling ball
a kind of tree found in Dayton
a kind of natural disaster
the age you should be allowed to vote

Sample Doppelganger Questions (continued)

the name of a planet
a restaurant within three miles of this library
the title of a book that has wizards in it
a gemstone used in jewelry
a kind of insect that makes you itch
the best excuse for not having homework
a high paying career
a low paying career
a color on a stoplight
a brand of underwear
an amusement park ride that goes way up
a kind of fruit that squirts when you eat it
the worst place to spend vacation
a cookie with chocolate in it
the age of a middle aged person
a flower that blooms in the spring
a winter holiday
the name of a soft drink or pop
a course you study in school
a common wattage for a light bulb
something you find in a house that has glass in it
a woman's shoe size
the name of a professional basketball player
a kind of cat you find in the zoo
something you use a remote control for
something you can lay down on outside
a street that crosses the one this library is on
a kind of operation many children have
a color of a rose
the name of a famous duo
a Christmas carol
the name of a kind of makeup (not a brand)
an afterschool activity
a really cool website
something you say "excuse me" for
a hospital in the Greater Dayton area
something you put on your hair
a movie starring Ben Efflec
something you plug into your TV system
something you do every day at school
the name of a saint
a rap artist
a country in Europe

Sample Doppelganger Questions *(continued)*
a food that is hard to wash off dishes once it dries
a store that sells virtually everything
the name of a wife of a U.S. President
a county that borders Montgomery County
something that sheds
the name of a military hero
an eating utensil
a nursery rhyme character
a religious denomination
something you toast
someone who wears a uniform
a kind of metal
some kind of tape
a water sport
a prime time TV cartoon character
something you take on your vacation
an occasion when a man should send flowers to his wife
a store that sells CDs
something you read that is not a book
a well-known Easter symbol
a country and western musician
something you find on a well stocked desk
a dairy food that does not come in a bottle
the name of one of the Beatles
a color in the American Flag
a food you peel before you eat it
the name of someone famous who died in the last year
something you see in the sky at night
something you use a boat for
a sport that requires participants to use a helmet
a TV comedian
a kind of SUV
two colors that go well together
something you hide under your bed
a vegetable that grows in most Ohio gardens
a kind of fluid you find in every car
a Jewish holiday
a kind of rock
something you should always have on you
an instrument you hear in jazz music
a kind of snack cracker
a famous brand of clothing

Figure 7.3 A list of Doppelganger questions.

Sample Lock-in Permission Slip

Parents:

Please print legibly! This Permission Slip must be completed and signed for each student attending the Lock-In on <u>DATE</u> and <u>TIME</u> for grades 7 - 12. No one will be admitted after <u>TIME</u>. No one will be permitted to leave the library until <u>TIME</u>. Library staff members will be in the building at all times and may be contacted at <u>PHONE</u>.

I give my daughter/son, _____,
permission to participate in the Library Lock-In on <u>DATE</u>.
During this activity, I, _____, can be
reached at (Phone) _____.

Emergency contact (other than above): The following adult is authorized to act in my behalf:
Name _____ Phone _____
Relationship to daughter/son _____
Physician _____ Phone _____
Hospital _____ Phone _____
I agree to the above.
Parent/Guardian Signature _____ Date _____
Teen Signature _____ Date _____

Your teen will need to bring:

Figure 7.4 A sample lock-in permission slip.

- Wear comfy clothes: no changing.
- Stay on one floor of the library.
- Separate sleeping rooms for boys and girls.
- Parents pick up teens unless they can drive themselves.

Teens are invited to bring a snack to share and the library provides pizza and pop. The remaining time is unstructured activities: board games, Internet, movies, video games (some of the boys bring their own game boxes), and the girls usually talk and read. Donuts and juice are served in the morning. Three to four staff members stay awake all night and parents help carpool to the theatre and back.

Time	Activity	Who is Responsible	What We'll Need
6:30 p.m.	Arrival; set aside personal gear; refrigerate snacks, if necessary	Lisa & Olivia; TAB members	refrigerator space location to place "gear": along wall of meeting room?
6:45 – 7:45	TAB Business meeting for December	Chair: Elizabeth Notetaker: need volunteer	agenda from Olivia & Lisa
7:45 – 8:30	Scavenger Hunt snack time	Elizabeth Kwiatkowski (with input from Keleigh, Meaghan, Colleen)	will arrive at 5 p.m. to set up; prizes for the winners! snacks from home
8:30 – 9:30	Radio-controlled (RC) cars in the stacks, over the children's room bridge, through the carpet creek, etc.	Olivia in cooperation with Adrienne and Brian Furness and the RC Club	bring an RC vehicle if we have one
9:30 – 10:30	Card game "Screw Your Neighbor" Other card games: your choice impromptu: magnetic poetry composition!	Adrienne Furness	UNO sets from children's dept. Decks of playing cards
10:30	Order pizza from Cam's NY Pizzeria (Ridge Road, 671-0180) Making a get well card for Colleen	Olivia Durant	card stock; markers; envelope
10:40	"Silent Stalking" with flashlights	Lisa Wemett	flashlights; OBIS kit with mini mag-lite
11:00	pizza; Who's Line is It Anyway?	Mindy	some scenarios we'll act out
11:30	Karaoke and DDR? "DWI: Dance with Intensity"	Lisa Wemett	borrow P.Deisinger's karaoke machine; TAB members bring music to share; library's stereo
12:30 a.m.	Movies: non-scary! (and scary?)PG-13	Olivia Durant	library's DVD player and projector; movie DVDs/ VHS

Figure 7.5 A lock-in schedule should include a few back-up activities in case the teens don't get into the first idea.

Time	Activity	Who is Responsible	What We'll Need
2 to 7 a.m.	Quiet time: Rule— don't have to sleep but you need to respect quiet time for others: Board games? Movies?		ideas for loan: Disney charades; Disney trivia; Twister; Moods
7:30	Anybody awake? Pack up personal belongings		
8:00	Breakfast offerings	Olivia and Lisa	
8:30	Departure		

Figure 7.5 *(continued)*

The Bottom Line

The Friends of the Library buys the pizza, the library buys the soda and juice, and a local bakery donates the donuts. The teens buy their discounted tickets to the movie.

Teen Feedback

Katie: "We should have a lock-in every month!" Teens love them.

TAB LIBRARY LOCK-IN, BY OLIVIA S. DURANT

Olivia invites her TAB members to the library for a lock-in as a thank-you for the work they've done over the year. The TAB plans the activities and timeline for the lock-in. The teens arrive on Saturday night at 6:30, bringing sleeping bags and snacks. When everyone is assembled, they have a regular TAB business meeting.

At one lock-in, one of the members conducted a scavenger hunt, sending teams around the library with clues. Afterwards, members of a local RC car club visited. They did stunt runs in the wide-open central space of the library and let the TAB members have some hands-on fun. In the next time block, our children's librarian taught them the card game "Screw Your Neighbor."

A new magnetic surface framed for the Teen Lounge provided entertainment for teen poets using magnetic poetry sets. While waiting for pizza to arrive, they played a game called "Silent Stalking," flashlight tag where "It" is blindfolded as the other players try to sneak up to him or her undetected.

After the pizza break, one of the members conducted a game of "Whose Line Is It Anyway?" with the chaperones.

As things started to wind down, TAB members were allowed to use the Internet computers for as long as they wanted. There was an impromptu session of Hide and Go Seek and there was a movie in the meeting room. A quiet-time rule began at 2 a.m. At around 3 a.m., a Playstation 2 was produced, along with a game called Dance Dance Revolution, which several teens played. Some stayed on the computers most of the early morning, and then bedtime finally happened around 5 a.m., with wake-up calls at 7:30 a.m. The bleary-eyed teens had some breakfast and were picked up by their parents between 8:30 and 9 a.m.

You will need flashlights, food, movies, a multimedia projector, a TV and VCR, board games, and other supplies for the activities the members plan. If each group of teens decides beforehand what activities they want to do, the supervisors can make their own list of supplies. Olivia also informed the police department that they would be at the library overnight.

Collection Connection

After the TAB's business meeting, the teens logged on to a bookstore Web site to print out their personal recommendations for DVDs and music recordings for the library to buy.

The Bottom Line

The expenses were the pizza and breakfast (e.g., juice, bagels, cream cheese). Parents may be willing to bring breakfast.

Teen Feedback

The teens completed evaluations about the lock-in:

What did you like about the sleepover?

- Lots of free time
- Hide and Go Seek
- Scavenger hunt; Elizabeth's hunt was the best! (3)
- Whose Line Is It Anyway?
- Games (2); card games
- Movies
- Rolling/spinning chairs
- Radio-controlled cars (2)
- Lots of activities: we had lots to do to keep busy

What could we do better?

- Start really early.
- Offer other choices at same time periods.
- Allow even more free time.
- Fix the DVD player. (3)
- Force more people to come.
- Turn off all the lights. (2)
- Offer a breakfast that folks would eat. [Editorial note: not too many folks ate what had been requested.]
- Do improv earlier: people were tired, winding down.
- Offer more after-hours activities.
- Encourage more TAB members to attend.
- From non-attendees: be able to bring a guest—more people to play games! Any kind of active stuff floats my boat (until about 11:30 p.m.).

Ideas for alternate activities at next sleepover:

- Pictionary
- Charades (2)
- Whose Line Is It Anyway?
- Name That Tune
- Board games: Moods, Scene It, etc.; board-game hour (3)
- Twister (2)
- One hour or half hour reading built in
- Hide and Seek
- Truth or Dare!

MARDI GRAS BASH,
BY KRISTIN FLETCHER-SPEAR AND KAREN REED

An after-hours evening of Mardi Gras fun attracted teens to Kristin and Karen's library. Two librarians and five teen volunteers ran this program. The program began with an original mystery written by Kristin and Karen, "The Mardi Gras Mystery," printed later in this section. When they wrote the mystery, they read a lot of books and studied maps of the New Orleans area. Teens from the Teen Library Council played the four suspects. The teens then gathered in teams of three to four to figure out who lied when being questioned by searching for the facts in the suspects' statements. This takes about half an hour. Almost everyone solved the mystery, which Kristin called the "admission into the real party."

Once in the programming room, the teens were given authentic Mardi Gras beads collected by a friend who lives in New Orleans. (You might need to order beads from Oriental Trading at www.orientaltrading.com.) At the party there was New Orleans–style music playing and tables set up with activities run by teens from the Teen Library Council: face painting, mask making, and the best—the bead table.

At the bead table, teens had to pull a card out of the Box of Humiliation and perform the task in order to get more beads. Some examples of the humiliation tasks are:

- Give someone a piggyback ride for five minutes.
- Wear a kick-me sign for ten minutes.
- Propose marriage to someone (Kristen was asked twice).
- Pretend to be Superman and fly around wearing a red cape.

They soon learned that these teens would beg, plead, and crawl on their knees for more beads!

After a while, the teens went back into the library to perform an Internet Scavenger Hunt about New Orleans. The New Orleans Scavenger Hunt is printed later in this section. Everyone received coins from Mardi Gras with Nicolas Cage's face on them for completing the hunt. Then they went to the program room and had King Cakes with the baby included. Kristen recommends warning the teens about the baby in the cake so no one will choke. Kristen and Karen searched online for King Cake recipes, but since King Cakes are much like coffee cakes, they ordered a festive cake from a bakery. The girl who won by finding the baby was informed that she would get to host the next party!

Collection Connection

Teens had to use books for the answers to the mystery and the Internet for the answers in the scavenger hunt.

The Bottom Line

Buy the face-painting kits on sale right after Halloween; Kristin spent only $10.00 for hers. The mask-making table included feathers, sequins, masks, string, and glue totaling about $25.00 or $30.00. The Cake was $45.00 and they served soda and chips. For their after-hours programs they usually allot between $150.00 and $200.00.

Teen Feedback

Kristin has some teens who always ask when the next after-hours party is going to be.

The Mardi Gras Mystery

Rules: Teens break into groups and are given the statements of the suspects. The suspect who is lying in his or her statement is the murderer. Books are used to check the facts in the suspect statements.

Scene: The masquerade ball was in full swing on Mardi Gras night. The bands were playing. The crowds were dancing. King Rex sat before them on his throne. With everyone in costume, best friends and mortal enemies wouldn't recognize each other. Suddenly, in the middle of the band's song, the lights went out. For a moment, it was mayhem. Women were screaming. Men were laughing. An entire tray of King Cakes hit the floor. When the lights were restored, King Rex lay dead on his throne strangled with his own Mardi Gras beads!

The Crime: King Rex, strangled with his own Mardi Gras beads at the New Orleans Masquerade Ball.

The Suspects: Two men and two women, each with a separate reason to dislike the victim, but who disliked him enough to kill him?

- Suspect 1, Theodore Thibodeaux (read by narrator): Theodore Thibodeaux, an up-and-coming candidate for mayor, was born with a silver spoon in his mouth in Thibodeaux, Louisiana, in the year John F. Kennedy was assassinated. A natural leader, he excelled in school and sports and quickly entered into politics after graduating from college. Nothing stained his immaculate record until King Rex's editorial on missing funds from the city's speeding-ticket till.

  Suspect 1 reads: "Well, it's a tragedy, there's no other word for it. We're going to miss old Rex's tenacious editorials. Look how he addressed that whole speeding-ticket fund fiasco. Thanks to Rex, we're investigating the matter thoroughly. Besides, I was nowhere near Rex at the time of the crime. I was on the balcony with one of my aides putting the last touch of my plans to renovate the land around Lake Maurepas into high-cost living for the segment of our population that I feel needs it most—the rich! Instead of wasting time interrogating me, maybe you should check out Annie Wheat. She was pretty upset when Rex exposed her blatant plagiarism. It ruined her reputation, after all! Besides, I'm Rex's first cousin. Why would I hurt my own family? Rex wasn't always scandal free himself. Remember that Boudreaux business twenty-something years ago?"

- Suspect 2, Raven LaVeaux (read by the narrator): A young woman, shrouded in mystery, this voodoo priestess has long been said to have a soul as dark as her eyes are brown. A longtime enemy of King Rex, twentysomething Raven hated the way Rex constantly belittled her religious beliefs. On more than one occasion, severed chicken parts were found on the front porch of Rex's spacious condominium. Though no evidence was ever found, most people pointed the finger straight at Raven. Just days before his death, Rex published another scathing article, criticizing voodoo practices. Born near Devil's Backbone in the year George W. Bush married his wife, Laura, Raven grew up in Buddha, Indiana, in a two-room shack, raised by her grandmother. Raven hated the small-town life and fled to New Orleans as soon as she turned 18.

Suspect 2 reads: "Yes, I hated him. The arrogant, self-righteous, pompous . . . but it is bad luck to speak ill of the dead . . . . Although I hated King Rex, I did not kill him. I've been training in the arts of voodoo for too long to waste my time with murder, especially one performed so crudely. When the lights went out, I was talking to Annie Wheat about the book *Tales of the Dead* by Bill Pronzini. For a moment, everyone panicked in the blackness. When the lights came on, Annie Wheat was nowhere to be found and the wretched King Rex was dead."

- Suspect 3, Annie Wheat (read by narrator): Once a well-respected popular writer of vampire and horror tales, Annie Wheat fell from grace after King Rex exposed her most recent work to be a thinly veiled plagiarism of Ambrose Bierce's *The Devil's Dictionary*. Annie took a beating in the press and sales of her *Satan's Thesaurus* plummeted. Born in the year Pearl Harbor was attacked, Annie Wheat grew up in the French Quarter of New Orleans above what is now called the Dungeon on Bourbon Street.

Suspect 3 reads: "I know everyone thinks I absolutely hated King Rex, but really, what harm did he do me? So I borrowed a little from Ambrose Bierce. It's not like anyone reads him anyway. Besides, *Satan's Thesaurus* is more of an elaboration than true plagiarism. When the lights went out, I was trapped in a tedious conversation with this horrid voodoo priestess named Raven about some boring book. I don't understand why people insist on telling me about third-rate authors. I'd much rather read "Murders on the Rue Morgue" by Edgar Allan Poe than the work of any contemporary writers. Sometimes I think I'm the only living writer with any talent at all! When the lights went out, I took my opportunity to slip away from Raven. The next thing I knew, King Rex was dead, but I had nothing to do with it. I suggest you turn your attention to Rex's latest victim of yellow journalism, the poor musician he tore to shreds in this week's music review column. Did you see the look on his face when King Rex's body was found? It struck me then, that young man is a dead ringer for King Rex himself."

- Suspect 4, Alexander Boudreaux (read by narrator): An aspiring jazz musician, 23-year-old Alexander Boudreaux was a one-hit wonder. At least, he was a one-hit wonder for one week. Then King Rex's scathing review robbed Boudreaux of the few loyal listeners he had. Alexander was born in New Orleans the year of the Bay of Pigs invasion. His mother died in childbirth and no father ever stepped forward to claim young Alexander. An unloving and distant aunt in Paris, Arizona, raised him. When he turned 20, he returned to New Orleans to seek his father, whom he had been told was a figure of some importance.

Suspect 4 reads: "When the lights went out, I was standing near the stage, strumming my guitar. I was hoping to provide some entertainment for the party, but thanks to King Rex, no one was interested in hearing me play. Just a few minutes before the murder, I'd been talking to Theodore Thibodeaux. He knew my mother, and I thought he'd know my dad. Thibodeaux got upset and wouldn't answer my questions. He said he wouldn't talk to any Boudreaux. I never used to get this feud between the families, but now I know why my dad never claimed me. That's a pretty lousy thing for a dad to do. . . . The only thing worse is, well . . . it doesn't matter. I plan on going to Chicago—that's where Charlie Parker was born. I think it should bring me good luck."

The Solution to the Mystery

- Suspect 1, Theodore Thibodeaux: The year John F. Kennedy was assassinated was 1963. That made Theodore 39 years old. Thibodeaux, Louisiana, really exists. Lake Maurepas really exists in Louisiana. While King Rex's editorial may have incriminated Theodore, he is still innocent of murder.
- Suspect 2, Raven LaVeaux: Devil's Backbone is a spot of interest in the southern part of Indiana. The year George W. Bush married his wife was 1977. That would make Raven in her twenties. Buddha, Indiana, is a real place. The book, *Tales of the Dead* by Bill Pronzini, is a real book.
- Suspect 3, Annie Wheat: Ambrose Bierce's *The Devil's Dictionary* is a real book. The year Pearl Harbor was attacked was 1941. Annie Wheat was 61 years old. Annie Wheat could read "Murders in the Rue Morgue" by Edgar Allan Poe because it is a real short story.
- Suspect 4, Alexander Boudreaux: If Alexander was born in New Orleans the year of the Bay of Pigs invasion, he would have been 41 years old, a discrepancy with his story. Paris, Arizona, does not exist. What else is he lying about? Charlie Parker was not born in Chicago; he was born in Kansas City, Missouri.

Alexander Boudreaux is the murderer. His motive? Being disowned at birth by his father, none other than the vitriolic King Rex. Abandonment was hard enough, but when King Rex dissed his music career, Alexander was pushed over the edge!

New Orleans Internet Hunt

Pair up with a friend or work by yourself to find an answer to each of the following questions. You may only use the Internet!

1. What in the world is a beignet? And what place in New Orleans is famous for them?
2. What famous vampire author lives in New Orleans?
3. In the history of Mardi Gras, what was the name of the first official Krewe formed?
4. What instrument did New Orleans native Harry Connick Jr. first learn to play?
5. Who was Marie LeVeaux?
6. Where is New Orleans?
7. What are the official colors of Mardi Gras?
8. When does the Mardi Gras carnival season begin officially?
9. When does Mardi Gras officially end?
10. Find a crawfish recipe and write it out.

Answers for the New Orleans Internet Hunt

1. A beignet is a square piece of dough, fried in vegetable oil and lavishly covered with powdered sugar. Café du Monde.
2. Anne Rice.
3. Mystick Krewe of Comus.
4. Piano.
5. New Orleans's most famous Voodoo Practitioner (Voodoo Queen).
6. In southeastern Louisiana.
7. Gold, purple, green.
8. January 6.
9. Forty-six days before Easter. Always the Tuesday before Ash Wednesday.
10. Multiple possibilities.

LOUD AT THE LIBRARY, BY AMY ACKERMAN AND LORA FEGLEY

A large community room and good sound equipment are prerequisites for a band concert at the library. Libraries that have held concerts are very pleased with the results as they attract large numbers of teens. Amy hoped to attract older teens who may never have participated in a library program before. The concert was held on a Friday night from 7 p.m. to 11 p.m. Amy invited four local bands to perform.

To set up, clear the area of tables and chairs, help the bands with their sound equipment, set up tables outside with ice, cups, and beverages and trash receptacles.

Five staff from the library system, nine staff from Parks and Recreation and the Boys and Girls Club, and one security officer kept things in order while over 200 teens danced and swayed the night away. Four of the guys from Parks and Recreation were former football players, so they got to break up mosh pits and do general front-stage damage control. One staff member from the library and one from Parks and Recreation served the drinks. One guy from the library guarded the gate into the rest of the library and did periodic restroom checks. Everyone else roamed the entire premises.

Amy gives these tips for a successful band concert at the library:

1. Get former football players who aren't afraid to jump into mosh pits or bellow intimidatingly.
2. Hire security. Most of the offenses happen in the parking lot, and you will be too busy to keep an eye on it. Amy had one officer, but is thinking of hiring at least one more for the next event.
3. Insist that everyone keep his or her drinks outside. Set up a table with the drinks just outside the entrance with garbage cans everywhere. Any spills will be kept outside, not on the carpet, and cleanup is a breeze.
4. Keep at least one staff member immediately accessible to parents dropping off kids. For the first hour, Amy found that the staff was mostly reassuring parents that it was going to be okay. A strong staff presence (and the cop car out front in the parking lot) really comforted a lot of parents.
5. Have fun! The teens will love it because the show and the drinks are free. Those who attended Amy's concert were surprised by that and acted like really gracious guests towards the workers.
6. Last but not least, wear comfortable shoes! Amy was on her feet for about six and a half hours straight.

The Bottom Line

The drinks cost $50.00 and the bands played for free. Amy had some flyers up in the library, but for the most part, the bands preferred to publicize themselves.

NERD CORE, BY SPRING LEA HENRY

Teens who love role-playing games, fantasy, and science fiction meet twice a month with Spring Lea, who is a fan herself! Self-declared nerds, the teens enjoy several different activities at their meetings, including Dungeons & Dragons, Magic the Gathering, and Yu-Gi-Oh. At other meetings they might

Figure 7.6 Role-playing games, fantasy, and science fiction bring teens together to share their interests.

enjoy a movie, eat pizza, discuss fantasy and science fiction books, magazines, and movies, and even write a few stories of their own. As Spring Lea explains, this is really a library club with a specific theme. The meetings are after school from 3:15 to 5:00 p.m. and they have had a couple of all-day events.

The best resource for a club like Nerd Core is a librarian with interest in science fiction and fantasy. If you are going to play D&D, then you will need the dice and the rule books. The other games require the playing cards, figurines, etc. The movies require audiovisual equipment and a movie license. Spring Lea has been doing this program by herself, but it is getting difficult with the 20 to 25 teens who show up for every meeting. She recommends recruiting a helper for that many teens. Word of mouth has been the best tool to help Nerd Core grow to such a steady large group.

Collection Connection

The teens and Spring Lea exchange favorite titles all the time. She has added D&D manuals to the collection for check out and they are never on the shelves.

The Bottom Line

The pizza has been the only cost, and that came out of the regular programming budget. Pizza vendors will give a deep discount, so remember to ask!

Teen Feedback

Spring Lea talks about her group: "I had a teen tell me the other day, Yeah, like one of my friends at school wanted to come, but I was like, please don't because we're so big now! The teens just love this group. The D&D has been especially popular. One girl told me her math skills have even improved because of the calculations in the game. The rest are just really creative people who love the group storytelling experience. But the most feedback I get is about me personally. The teens really seem to like having an adult in their lives who shares their passion for science fiction and fantasy. Several have told me how weird they felt for liking this stuff before Nerd Core. It's like the group has given them permission to be themselves."

LYBRARY LYMPICS, BY CATHY HOCHADEL

Lybrary Lympics is a great low-cost way to get kids into the spirit of the Olympic Games. This is a noisy activity, so warn your staff and patrons that typical library decibel levels will be exceeded, or schedule an after-hours program. Do as many games outdoors as possible, if weather permits. You will need to recruit helpers to set up and clean up for a Lympic event. The program will take one to one and a half hours, depending on the number of games offered.

Lybrary Lympics generates a lot of interest because of the misspelling of the title of the program, the names of the games to be held, and the prizes that will be awarded. The first place prizes for each event are candy bars and/ or free ice cream coupons from a local Dairy Queen. The Grand Prize is awarded to the overall winner of the events, and can be something cool donated from a sporting goods store or something cheap and goofy like an action figure painted gold glued on top of a withdrawn or discarded paperback book.

You will need masking tape, damaged CDs, signs with rules printed on them for each game, a softball and one to three bean bags, library books as needed according to the descriptions of the games, and water or other beverages.

The games can be completed in any order. The participants must take a turn at each game to qualify for the Grand Prize. Describe the games to the kids, emphasizing the importance of following the rules posted by each game site. Explain that there will be a first-place prize for each event and that the Grand Prize will be awarded to the person with the most First Places. Cathy suggests buying a candy bar for each of your library aides who have to reshelve the books!

Sample Games and Set-up Instructions:

- Standing Book Jump: Lay ten books that are 12" in height end to end in a straight line; put a line of tape at one end behind which the contestant must stand to jump. Longest jump wins.
- Paperback Stack: Select books that will be allowed in the competition; pile them up. Tallest stack wins.
- CD Discus Toss: Set this up where traffic can be controlled; make the distance between where the contestant stands and the target approximately 20'. Warning: flying CDs can be dangerous so rope off the area and have someone posted who can keep the activity safe. Longest distance or closest to target wins.
- Paperback Bowling: A softball is a great bowling ball for this activity. Mark the distance between the foul line and the books approximately 12 to 15 feet with lines of masking tape. Set up ten paperbacks like pins at the bowling alley. Be sure to have an aide or volunteer stationed to remove and reset the "pins" as they're knocked down. Most pins down wins.
- Book Walk: Using masking tape, mark off the starting line, the finishing line, and the route that the contestant must walk carrying a book on his head. Place a strip of tape at the end of each range that must be crossed for the distance to be counted. A real challenge is to make the contestant "toe the line" on the tape, and to make the path windy and wavy—you may have to resort to this as you might have a couple of really flat-headed kids! Longest distance wins.
- Bean Bag Book Blast: Stand up five to six withdrawn books of varying sizes and thicknesses on a table or other flat surface. Using masking tape, mark off the foul line 12' away. Knock them down with bean bags. Most down wins.

Collection Connection

Display biographies of Olympic medalists, books on sports, sports videos, sports magazines, etc. Use YA books for the events.

Chapter 8

Programs for Girls

OVERVIEW

Sometimes girls just want to be girls, so why not have fun at the library enjoying all that's feminine? From indulging in makeup, hair styles, and fashion that make girls feel pretty on the outside, to exercises and projects that work on bringing out the beauty from inside, these programs will help your teen girls be more confident—looking and feeling better on the inside and the outside.

DIY BEAUTY, BY KRISTIN FLETCHER-SPEAR

Teen girls can learn how to make their own beauty products from ingredients from the kitchen in DIY Beauty. This one-and-a-half-hour program begins with a personal consultation quiz and a discussion about natural beauty products. The girls follow recipes to create a nail soak from pineapple juice and yogurt and a summer cleansing mask from sour cream and oatmeal. While everyone was having their faces masked, Kristin talked about mud, essential oils, and many of the other recipes that they had compiled for the teens. Throughout the evening, recipe sharing is interspersed with booktalks and more tips for healthy living. At the end of the night, Kristin made fruit smoothies for the teens.

Kristin gave the girls a 42-page booklet of recipes and other tips compiled from Web sites and books from the library's collection. The booklet was typed into a word document and is comb bound. The back cover lists Internet and print resources. You will need to bring in the foods you use for the recipes, towels, bowls to soak their hands in, and a blender if you are making smoothies.

DIY Beauty Booklet Table of Contents
Personal Consultation Quiz
Personal Consultation Quiz Results
Steps to Natural Beauty
Ten Ways of Dealing with Stress
Tips for Beauty
Ultimate Manicure
Fabulous Feet Pedicure
The Perfect Facial
DIY Beauty Recipes
Clay
Clay Recipes
Essential Oils Tips
Essential Oils
Essential Oil Recipes
Recipes to Eat
Escapism at Its Finest
Nonfiction Books
Books and Websites for more Information

Figure 8.1 Many beauty tips are included in the DIY Beauty Booklet

Collection Connection

The whole program was researched in the library's collection.

The Bottom Line

You can make this program as expensive or as cheap as you like. Kristin did it for $15.00 by using the same ingredients for different recipes.

Teen Feedback

The greatest compliment was when two of the girls asked Kristin a year and a half after the program when they'll be doing it again because they want their other friends to attend.

TEEN HOOPLA BOOK CLUB, BY AMANDA SPARGO

Girls between 12 and 15 meet with Amanda the last Monday of every month for an hour of great book discussion, popcorn, and cocoa or juice.

Amanda brings new teen fiction, book reviews, and recommended reading lists she has collected from Web sites. The girls bring a small notebook, a pen, and an open mind. For the next hour Amanda booktalks titles she

Figure 8.2 Being beautiful doesn't have to be all hard work!

has read and the girls jump in if it is a novel they have heard about or read themselves. The girls tell the group what they have been reading and everyone takes notes for good titles to read. At the end of the meetings each girl regularly signs out ten to 15 books for an extended loan period of four weeks until the next meeting.

Occasionally, the Teen Hoopla Book Club will interact with the two other Mother-Daughter Book Clubs Amanda leads when there is an author visit or a group outing, such as going to see a film based on a novel they have all read. At the end of each meeting there is a drawing for a free book. Amanda saves advance reading copies from publishers to use for the book drawings. Twice a year, Amanda shares advance copies with all the club members to review for purchase for the branch libraries.

Collection Connection

The book club booktalks promote the young adult collection and gives Amanda direct feedback from the teens, helping with collection development for the branch libraries.

The Bottom Line

The club goes through two bags of popcorn and one bottle of juice per meeting, averaging about $5.00 a month.

Teen Feedback

The program has proven to be very successful and a natural stepping stone for girls who have belonged to the Mother-Daughter Book Club. The MD clubs are for girls ages eight to ten and ten to twelve, and avid readers have a place to continue sharing fantastic reads past the age of 12. It has become a special time for these young women. The older girls often act as big sisters to younger girls, sharing must-reads with them.

FOR GIRLS ONLY!!, BY
BONNIE DEMARCHI AND LINDA STASKUS

Sixth- through twelfth-grade girls met after school for a series of six programs For Girls Only!! The first series was a six-week session, but when the weekly schedule proved to be tough for the staff to maintain, the following program series were held monthly. The programs were planned for an hour, but often lasted one and a half hours because the girls became so involved in the activities.

The For Girls Only!! program was developed because Bonnie and Linda felt there is a strong need to counteract the negative influences of society and the media on women, especially for young adolescent girls. The objectives were to instill in the girls self-awareness, feminine awareness, positive self-image, and the importance of healthy female friendships. Through activities and discussion the girls developed a sense of who they are and who they can be by being true to themselves and not succumbing to peer and media pressures. They did this while having lots of fun.

There are loose themes for each session. For many of the programs, women from the community presented the program: a mehndi artist, a makeup artist, a martial arts expert, yoga instructors, hair stylists, and a botanist, for example. Themes included:

- Personal safety: martial arts
- Body adornment: tattooing, piercing, mehndi
- "Friendship: Hot Topics for Teens," *Friends* video (www.rmcumc.org/ CR/RQM/rqm.cgi?resCode=V716=&detail=Y)
- Body image and advertising
- Creativity: women artists, art or craft project
- Fantasy: movie, books, decorating masks
- Journaling: handmade journals
- Problem solving: Problem Solver game (www.therapeuticresources.com/ problemdecision.html)
- Women's History: Women's Rights Movement
- Charm, etiquette, and poise

- Skin care and makeup tips
- Gardening
- Health and physical fitness: belly dancing, yoga

Collection Connection

Book discussions and booktalks relating to the theme were presented at each program. Relevant videos with public performance rights were shown. Bonnie and Linda also created bibliographies for fiction, nonfiction, poetry, biography, videos, professional development, and parents.

Teen Feedback

The girls loved the program. A few were members for several years until they outgrew the group.

PROM PREVIEW, BY LINDA UHLER

High school girls planning to attend their proms were invited to a Prom Preview at Linda's library. Ten teen girls volunteered to model prom gowns and three teen guys modeled tuxedoes. A makeup artist from a local department store did makeovers, and a local hair studio styled the models' hair. A bridal and prom shop brought two dresses, jewelry, shoes, wraps, and accessories for each girl.

One at a time, each model came out as the makeup artist talked about what products were used and the hair stylist described the hair style and why it was chosen. The prom shop representative then talked about the gown, how the style worked on the model's body type, what other colors were available, and the cost. The speakers talked about the current trends, as well as what's appropriate and what's not.

The three guys modeled the tuxes while the girls changed into their second gowns. The guys then escorted the girls to the front of the stage area. During the second modeling, only the gown was discussed.

Linda decorated with greenery borrowed from a local florist and served cookies and punch refreshments. Prom-related door prizes were given away, including gift certificates to restaurants, floral shops, jewelry boutiques, prom magazines, and donated hair products. A program announcing sponsors and models' names was given to the girls, moms, dads, and boyfriends who attended.

Collection Connection

Books were displayed on the following topics: teen beauty, makeup, dressing well for different body types, and teen etiquette.

Teen Feedback

The teens had loads of fun and want to do the program again!

FASHIONISTAS, BY KRISTINA DAILY

Girls attended a makeover program to celebrate Teen Read Week at Kristina's library. Three girls received complete makeovers, including haircut, color, style, and makeup during the afternoon before the program and eight more girls had their hair styled by local hairdressers and applied makeup with the assistance of a Mary Kay representative in front of the audience. Eighty-three people attended the program.

The room was divided into two areas. Four girls had their hair done while the other four were across the room receiving makeup instruction, and then the groups switched. The audience was free to watch the area that interested them.

After the makeovers were completed, there was a brief fashion show with the girls modeling their own clothing and a display of the complete makeovers. A raffle was held for door prizes from the participating hair salons and Mary Kay. Four local hairdressers and a Mary Kay representative donated their time for the program. The 11 models were teen volunteers, recruited to represent a variety of racial and ethnic backgrounds as well as hair types.

Collection Connection

Kristina's library updated the collections on hair care, beauty, and self-esteem. There was a materials display in the room featuring books and videos on hair, makeup, clothing, modeling, and self-esteem.

The Bottom Line

The hairdressers and Mary Kay representative donated their time but door prizes were purchased from their organizations to award at the event. The total program cost, including simple refreshments, was $300.00.

Teen Feedback

There was a lot of positive feedback from teens after the program. One of the models slept in a chair that night and did not change her shirt so her friends could see what she looked like at school the next morning. This program also led to new members at the next teen advisory board meeting. It was a very positive experience and the hairdressers were all interested in doing it again next year.

Chapter 9

Programs for Boys

OVERVIEW

I worked on a bookmobile for ten years prior to working in YA services. We served elementary schools and I regularly observed a very obvious change in reading habits between boys and girls around the fourth grade. The girls continued loving fiction, enjoying longer and longer novels about relationships between people, while the boys moved across the bookmobile into the nonfiction, where the text was broken up with graphics and the topics included monsters, dinosaurs, wild animals, and sports. The boys also liked the choose-your-own-adventure style of novels, where they had an active role in deciding how the story would end.

As boys get older the emphasis in literature classes in school is on novels, and since boys often tend to gravitate away from novels several years before they get into those classes, it appears that boys don't like to read. Yet, many librarians and moms can tell you that boys love graphic novels, magazines, the Internet, and reading about sports, video games, music, and just to make things more complicated, fantasy adventures.

So my observation has been that many boys love to read, just not always the same things girls like to read. As luck would have it, most librarians and literature teachers are female. If you have a problem getting boys into your library, getting them to read, or getting them to programs, take a look at what you are offering them. Interestingly, I get more boys in my TAB than girls, and they are more vocal about what they want me to add to the collection, while the girls are already reading what is in the collection.

Two recent helpful resources for planning library services for boys are Michael Sullivan's *Connecting Boys and Books: What Libraries Can Do* and ALA's Web page, BOYS WILL BE . . . The unique reading and development needs of boys in libraries at www.ala.org/ala/alsc/alscresources/forlibrarians/serviceboys/serviceboys.htm.

DEMO OF ADVENTURE ROLE-PLAYING GAMES, BY BRIAN SIMONS

While open to both genders, role-playing game programs attract more boys. Brian invites a local merchant who sells role-playing games to bring eight to fifteen games for teen guys to try. The merchant brings his own volunteers to help him set up the games. The games are whatever is new and popular at the time, such as Pokemon, Dungeons & Dragons, Mage Knight, Magic, Lord of the Rings, and Star Wars. Most of the games require an exorbitant amount of reading and rely on a very fertile imagination.

Some of the participants have never tried role-playing before and this is their introduction to the whole gaming culture; others have role-played, but they want to try new games or games they normally don't play. Both groups get a chance to have a new experience without making the financial commitment of buying the game pieces, books, or items.

Brian used many of the traditional avenues of publicity, but he also talked to various teachers and guidance counselors at the schools, some of whom gave extra credit to students who attended this program.

The teens are offered soda and snacks when they come in. The different games are set up all over the library meeting room, allowing enough space for five to ten players at each game. As each teen or group of teens comes in, they are invited to browse the games in progress and, if interested, sit down to join a game. The person leading the game explains the rules. The experienced gamers jump from one game to the next and then settle in to focus on the game of their choice.

Teens new to gaming usually need some explanation of what things are, and they mill around a bit before getting the courage to try a game. Brian helps them out by giving a little nudge when necessary, finding out which game someone thinks he'd like to try, bringing that teen over to the game, and introducing him to the game leader: "This is so and so, he'd like to try this game out. Do you have room for him?" They always have room but this breaks the ice for the timid teen; before you know it he is laughing and having a great time.

Since these games are based on imagination they could go on forever. Make an announcement 15 minutes before the end of the program so the players can wind things up. Brian's program is two hours long.

Collection Connection

Dungeons & Dragons books, Magic books and any other gaming books owned by the library can be displayed near the corresponding games. Gamers usually enjoy fantasy series, as well.

The Bottom Line

Brian spends about $30.00 to feed soda and chips to 44 teens. The game merchant does the program for free since it is essentially free advertising for him.

Teen Feedback

There is a perception, mainly due to some bad PR in the early 1980s, that these games are dangerous or that the people who play them are introverts. Once you host a program you'll see that the opposite is true. One teen thanked Brian for doing this program and wanted to know when they'd do it again. The teen further explained that his mom doesn't like him hanging out in the store (for the reasons mentioned above) but she was happy to let him come to the library for this event.

BOARD GAME COMPETITIONS BY ROSEMARY HONNOLD

Game tournaments seem to attract more boys than girls. The annual Monopoly™ tournament at Coshocton Public Library is a favorite with our teen guys. Games like chess, checkers, Risk,™ and Battleship™ are other favorites. The game tournaments give the boys new opponents to play against. You can promote other programs and library materials to your captive audience during breaks. Plan to have pizza or snacks during the program.

LAN PARTIES BY ROSEMARY HONNOLD

Computer gamers aren't always the solitary creatures we imagine them to be. It is much more fun to play computer games with human opponents and even better when you know your opponents. Friends combined with favorite computer games will attract boys to your computer lab for an exciting event. Some LAN (Local Access Network) parties last entire weekends, so you can schedule yours for a few hours or for an all night lock-in. Your library's computer lab may already be networked to accommodate gaming parties. To host a LAN party, you will need:

- At least six to eight networked computers positioned so the players will be able to see each other, but not see each others' screens.
- Headphones and joysticks, if needed.
- An adequate power system so no circuits will pop during play.
- Air conditioning to keep the room and computers comfortable.
- A copy of the game software for each computer. Some players will have their own copies they can bring to the party. Different games can be played by different clusters of players at the same party.
- Refreshments. Traditional LAN party food is pizza, chips, and soda.

Be sure to investigate the ratings of the games you plan to offer or host, and target the appropriate age group in the publicity. Some games have mature themes or graphic violence. You might consider requiring parental permission to attend the LAN party, with a list of the games that will be offered.

PROGRAM IDEAS FOR BOYS BY PATRICK JONES

In the following figure, Patrick Jones's list of subjects that boys like is arranged by Dewey subject. They're great starting places for more program ideas just for boys. Many of the programs in this book and in *101+ Teen Programs That Work* fit into these categories. Use this list at a TAB meeting to brainstorm more program ideas. If you wonder if guys will like a program idea, just ask them!

Subjects For Program Ideas
001 Guinness Book, UFOs, Computers, Newsletters, Web pages, Newspapers.
100 Parapsychology, Witchcraft, Hypnosis.
200 Cults
300 True crime, Reading tutors, Urban legends, Legal rights, Military, College selection, College tests, Careers, Stock market, Boy scout badge programs, Police/detective work, Prom fashion, College financial aid.
400 Slang
500 Science experiments, Rocketry, Astronomy, Animals.
600 Sex, Gay teens, Model cars, Sound systems, Robotics, Forensic science, Buying used cars, Low rider cars, Summer jobs, Motorcycles, Bicycles, Health issues, Airplanes, Sports cars.
700 Air brushing, Video production, Golf, ATVs, Theater, Acting, Comic books, Computer art, Graphic novels, Silk screening, Photography, Sports as career, Sports card collecting, Sci Fi movies, Art shows, Street dance, Radio personalities, Live music, Basketball, Baseball, Skateboarding demo, Bow hunting, Scooters, Paintball, Yo Yos, Football, Soccer, Magic the gathering, NASCAR, Weight lifting, Painting, Body art, Hunting, Role playing games, Slot car racing, Fishing, Camping, Survival skills, Computer games, Chess, Checkers, Drawing comics, Pro wrestling, Hockey, Martial arts, Snow boarding, Skiing, Boxing, Extreme sports, Card games, Horror movies.
800 Poetry, Research papers, Characters from sc-fi, Mystery nights, Book discussion sci -fi
900 Oral history, True adventure.

Figure 9–1 The library collection is a treasure trove of programming topics that boys will like. Patrick Jones has accumulated these ideas from his workshop attendees.

Chapter 10

Programs for Tweens

OVERVIEW

Tweens . . . the middle school students who don't want to be children anymore, but who aren't ready for the older teen crowd. Focusing on this age group with your programs will help corral their boisterous energy and steer it in a positive, constructive direction. You will also be nurturing future teen library lovers. Libraries with hordes of middle school students descending after school are finding many clever ways to make the most of this captive audience.

DON'T BUY THE ELEVATOR PASS: YOUR GUIDE TO MIDDLE SCHOOL, BY JENNIFER STENCEL

Sixth graders are invited to hear the wisdom of the more seasoned middle schoolers while munching on pizza. Jennifer schedules this 45-minute program a day or two after the school's orientation program so new sixth graders can ask the older students the real-deal questions about middle school.

Jennifer recruits seventh and eighth grade panelists throughout the summer. To try her program, begin with the students who are active in the summer reading program who are also active at school, and they in turn will ask their friends. Next, call the middle school principal the last week in July, and ask to set up a table at the school's orientation to promote the library as a resource for homework help and to promote this library program. Create a promotional display for the table at the school: a backpack full of books and school supplies with tickets arranged to flow out of the bag. The tickets are actually the program flyers with the date and time of the program and read "Don't Buy the Elevator Pass: Your Guide to Middle School." The parents get the joke before the teens and end up selling the program to their sixth graders.

A week before the program, contact a local pizza shop to send in an order for discounted pizzas. Gather cheap and fun school supplies at local grocery and drug stores—calculator key chains and glitter highlighters, for example—to use for door prizes. One half hour before the program, meet with the panelists to go over the organization of the program, urging them to be understanding of the questions they may get from the petrified sixth graders.

Jennifer organized the discussion into four categories to help move things along:

- Teachers, Classes, and Homework
- Social "Seen": Hallways to Pep Rallies and Dances
- Extra Stuff: Student Council to Sports
- Panelist Horror Stories: each panelist tells the sixth graders an embarrassing story or situation that happened to him or her (the sixth graders love this, as it makes the seventh and eighth graders more human)

After the panel and questions and answers, everyone is invited to sit around, munch on pizza, and visit.

Collection Connection

Erlbach, Arlene and Helen Flook. 2003. *Middle School Survival Guide*. New York: Walker & Company.

Farrell, Juliana and Beth Mayall. 2001. *Middle School: The Real Deal: From Cafeteria Food to Combination Locks*. New York, NY: HaperCollins

Morgenstern, Julie and Jesse Morgenstern-Colon. 2002. *Organizing from the Inside Out for Teens*. New York: H. Holt.

Mosatche, Harriet. 2000. *Too Old for This, Too Young for That!: Your Survival Guide for the Middle-School Years*. Minneapolis, MN: Free Spirit

Weston, Carol. *For Teens Only: Quotes, Notes, and Advice You Can Use*. Harper Trophy; 1st Harper Trophy ed.

The Bottom Line

The Friends of the Richfield Library support this program, which costs no more than $20.00 total for door prizes and pizza, pop, and paper products.

Teen Feedback

Since Jennifer started this program, parents and teens ask if she is going to do it again the following year. Both parties have said it was a great help; they could ask the questions that really mattered and get honest feedback from those who have recently gone through it all. The school-sponsored event is more of an open house (teachers need not be present): here is a map with your schedule, here is your locker, here is the dress code, etc. The sixth graders want to get the inside scoop, the heads-up before they walk through the doors for the first time. Once the sixth graders go through "Don't Buy the Elevator Pass" they want to be on the panel for the next year. Each year it is growing from word of mouth!

CHINESE POSTCARDS, BY MELISSA PILLOT

While this program can be adapted to other countries or cultures, the example here features China. Middle schoolers arrive after school to learn about the Chinese culture by looking at artifacts that represent the country. Collect and display five to ten Chinese items: a stuffed panda, an abacus, a yin-yang symbol, and chopsticks, for example. Prepare short summaries about each item. Invite the students to take a look at all the Chinese items in the room. Tell them some facts from the summaries and demonstrate each item individually, or allow the participants to browse the room on their own and read the summaries. If the latter approach is taken, ask the participants to tell you about one or two things they saw.

Collect the following items for up to 20 students:

- 20 blank postcards
- 20 postcard stamps
- 20 fortune cookies
- Colored pencils
- Chinese character rubber stamps and ink pads
- Pencils and pens

Give each participant a blank postcard so he or she can draw one of the artifacts seen on the trip around the room. Bring the artifacts to the drawing table so they can make an accurate drawing. They might also use the Chinese character stamps to put words on the card.

Demonstrate the proper way to write and address a postcard. Have the participants draw a line down the middle of the back of their postcard. They should write a short note on the left-hand side of the line, then address it to someone (friend, family member, themselves) on the right-hand side. When a participant presents the postcard to the instructor, he or she receives a stamp in order to actually mail the card. If time and materials permit, let everyone do a second postcard. Give each participant a fortune cookie at the end.

Collection Connection

Frost, Helen. 2001. *A Look at China.* Mankato, MN: Capstone Press.
Hill, Valerie. 2003. *Ask About Asia: China.* Broomall, PA: Mason Crest Publishers (February 1).
Salas, Laura Purdie. 2001. *Countries and Cultures: China.* Mankato, MN: Capstone Press.

Wang, Tao. 1995. *Exploration into China.* New York: New Discovery Books (August 1).

Whiteford, Gary T. 2002. *China.* Philadelphia, PA: Chelsea House Publications (August 1).

The Bottom Line

The postcards were $20.00 for 200, Chinese character stamps were $20.00 from the Art Museum Store, fortune cookies were $15.00 for a case of 240, and postcard stamps were $23.00. The total cost was $78.00 for 100 kids at seven branches.

Teen Feedback

The young teens were really excited that they actually got to mail their postcards. There were some fantastic designs, and they loved learning the meanings for the Chinese characters.

READING RANTS: A BOOKTALKING PROGRAM FOR MIDDLE SCHOOLERS, BY KELLY LASZCZAK

Reading Rants is a booktalking program that Kelly's library takes to the middle schools. Two librarians visit the schools in the fall and again in the spring to booktalk to every English class in all three grades. Letters are sent to the English teachers to remind them to schedule a time through the school librarians. Their booktalks take an entire class period.

The librarians compile a list of 40 to 60 recent books for middle school readers. They include a variety of genres, fiction and nonfiction, titles for boys and girls. The visiting librarians each read half of the books on the list.

In the classroom, the librarians introduce themselves and explain why they are visiting the school; each speaks about one of the books. After that, the students raise a hand to choose the next titles for them to discuss. The talks last two to three minutes each and they cover 12 to 15 titles per class period.

Every book on the Reading Rants list receives a read-alike label inside the back cover. Four read-alike titles are printed on the labels, using a word-processing program. Surveys may be included in the program. The students give their opinions about music, books, and Web sites.

Collection Connection

Books for Reading Rants are chosen from the young adult and the juvenile collections. Statistics show that this type of promotion of the entire collection increases the circulation of the titles.

Did you like
Sword of the Rightful King by Jane Yolen?
You may like these books:

Forbidden Forest
by Michael Cadnum

Seeing Stone
by Kevin Crossley-Holland

The Winter Prince
by Elizabeth Wein

Girl in a Cage
by Jane Yolen

Recommended by the
Youth Services Librarians of the Hinsdale Public Library.

**Figure 10.1 Read-alike labels guide young people
to more books they might enjoy.**

The Bottom Line

Paper for booklists and labels for the read-alike lists are the only expense.

Teen Feedback

The student and teacher response is always very positive. Teachers' comments include: "It's always so great to hear about new books for kids." "We always enjoy hearing you talk." "This is the students' favorite day." The students are always eager to choose books and to hear about the Reading Rants list. Comments from the students include: "Yes! The librarians are here!" "I want to read a lot of the books on this list." "Can I take books home today?"

THE KEARNS TEEN PROGRAM, BY TRISH HULL

The Kearns Teen Program is one of the 25 winners of YALSA's 2004 Excellence in Service to Young Adults Recognition Project. Trish's library attracts 50 to 100 junior high students every day after school. There had been a lot of vandalism, disrespectful behavior, fighting, and police intervention. The library decided to provide an activity every Thursday after school to help the kids connect the library with people who care and can help them.

The library has organized crafts, parties, speakers, dancers, skateboard tips, and harmonica lessons among many other activities. They invite anyone they can recruit to do a program—like the local hockey-team ice dancer who taught the kids a dance. When the students come into the library, they are steered towards the auditorium and given a snack. They are supervised by one librarian and one or two interns, as needed. The students are low-income, racially and ethnically diverse, at-risk, latchkey kids who hang around the library for several hours after school. The program is not promoted outside the library, as it is for the kids who walk in the door.

The Bottom Line

The expenses vary and some of the programs can be expensive, but often they are free. The end of the school year pizza party cost $100.00. The library received a $1,000.00 grant from Wal-Mart for a literacy program and the YALSA award, which has helped finance the program. The library also asks for donations and utilizes its own resources.

Teen Feedback

The teens always comment on the programs. Sometimes "it sucks" and other times they want "those guys [whoever they were that week] to come back!" The best comment Trish has heard about the program was when her daughter saw two boys running into the library saying, "Hurry, we're late!" and she realized they were coming to the teen activity.

GIRLS ONLY AND BOYS' NIGHT, BY ALISON MILLER

The girls and the boys have their own special times to meet each month at Alison's library. Alison runs the Girls Only program and her husband (a teacher and a library volunteer) runs the Boys' Night program. The groups meet for two hours.

They usually start out with a guest speaker followed by a discussion or activity. If they do not have a guest speaker, they begin with an activity or discussion that involves the monthly theme, based on books or holidays. During the second hour, they do crafts, play games, and have refreshments. Most of the resources are available at the library and the guest speaker may also bring something.

Collection Connection

Alison gathers books related to the group topic.

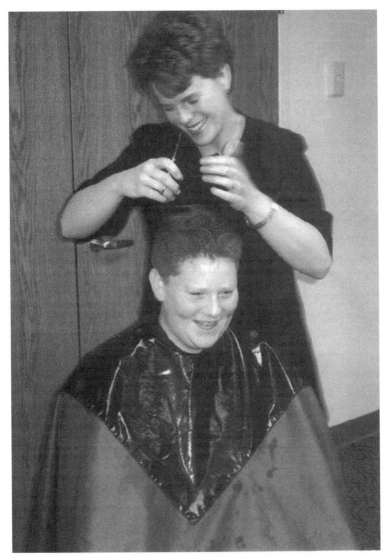

**Figure 10.2 Boy and girl teens enjoyed getting
a makeover at the library.**

The Bottom Line

Expenses are low: the refreshments are provided by the library staff and the speakers volunteer.

Teen Feedback

The kids enjoy themselves and they often ask, "Why can't we have a girls' and boys' night every week?"

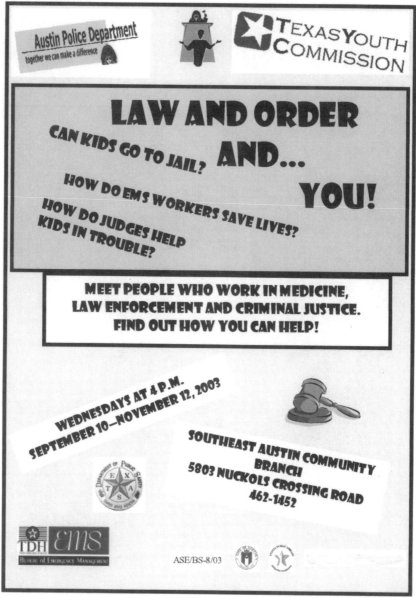

Figure 10.3 The promotional poster for Law and Order and ...You!

TEEN MAKEOVER, BY DEB BELEW

A local hairdresser volunteered to give twelve teens a makeover at Deb's Library. Eight girls and four boys received free samples of hair products and heard tips on hygiene and makeup techniques for early teens. They got haircuts, highlights, and new styles. The hairdresser also coached them about hair products for different hair types. If you do a makeover program, you will need lots of towels, music, and snacks.

The Bottom Line

The hairdresser donated her services. The snacks and pizza were $20.00.

Teen Feedback

The teens loved the program; there was lots of laughter and silliness.

LAW AND ORDER AND ...YOU!, BY BETH SOLOMON

Beth's library hosted a ten-week series of programs for middle schoolers with speakers from state and local agencies concerned with public safety and the law. To find speakers, Beth contacted the Prevention Director of the Texas Youth Commission, who gave her suggestions and contact information for presenters. The one-hour programs feature criminal justice, emergency medical services, underage-drinking prevention, and law enforcement. The agencies were eager to participate and willing to present more than once on different topics. The presenters brought their own props and visual aids, such as a video or medical equipment. Each student received a small package of cookies or snack crackers on the way into the program, and one half of a numbered ticket for the two door prizes at each session ($5.00 gift cards to a local fast-food restaurant or Wal-Mart). Those who remained through the end of the day's program were eligible to win the door prizes.

Beth recommends having an adult at the door, as the students may tend to wander in and out, which is distracting. The attendees helped give out the snacks and draw the winning numbers for the door prizes. After the program, send a thank-you note to the presenter.

Collection Connection

Books on relevant subjects were on display because most of the students spent the afternoon in the library after the program.

The Bottom Line

Snacks and door prizes are the only expenses. The food was donated by a local grocery chain, H.E.B., and the door prizes provided by grant funds from the Michael and Susan Dell Foundation, through Youth Services at the Austin Public Library.

Wednesdays, 4 p.m.	WHO	WHAT
September 10 www.ci.austin.tx.us/ ems/default.htm	Anna Sabana Dept. of Public Safety, EMS 476-1552	Paramedics will demonstrate how they save lives. Learn how you can become a life-saver.
September 17 www.co.travis.tx.us/ county_attorney/ Underage_Drinking_Pgm/ default.asp	Gloria Souhami Travis Co. Underage Drinking Prevention Program 854-4229	Representative from this program will show a video made at Gardner-Betts Juvenile Justice Center, "Busted," exploring the legal consequences of underage drinking.
September 24	Gloria Souhami Travis Co. Underage Drinking Prevention Program 854-4229	This program uses special goggles and interactive exercises to give kids a first-hand understanding of the health hazards of underage drinking.
October 1 Texas Youth Commission **Prevention:** Dr. Tracy Levins phone: 512-424-6336 email: prevention@tyc.state.tx.us www.tyc.state.tx.us/	Residents from Thurman House, a Halfway House run by the Texas Youth Commission Contact: Laurie Westfall 452-6481	Meet kids who have successfully completed the Rehabilitation Program with the Texas Youth Commission. Hear how they are turning their lives around.
October 8 www.co.travis.tx.us/ juvenile_court/default.asp	Brian Snyder, Director of Detention Services, Gardner Betts Juvenile Justice Center 854-7000 (former co-worker of Dana McBee, APL Finance Officer)	The Directors of Detention, Court and Probation Services at Gardner-Betts bring you the real deal on what happens when kids break the law in Austin.
October 22 www.oag.state.tx.us/ criminal/cluzine/ cluconsp.htm	Tammy Schroeder, contact at the Texas State Attorney General's Office 475-0422 Moderated by APL Finance Office and former Probation Officer Dana McBee	We will view a "Consequences Curriculum" video, filmed at Gardner-Betts, detailing the real life consequences of breaking the law.
October 29 www.swcapt.org/ science.html and www.texans standingtall.com/ newpolicy2.html#01	Julie Stevens, Texas State Liaison for the Southwest Center for the Application of Prevention Technology 349-6634	Representatives of this initiative will present a hands-on workshop training kids to deconstruct media ads and commercials. Learn how to NOT let your values be manipulated, a key step in making the right behavior decisions.

Wednesdays, 4 p.m.	WHO	WHAT
October 15 (*change) www.ci.austin.tx.us/police/ default.htm or www.ci.austin.tx.us/fire/ default.htm	Southwest Neighborhood Liaison, Austin Police Department or Austin Fire Department	Details to be announced.
November 5 (*change) www.co.travis.tx.us/ district_courts/civil_courts/ 98.asp	The Honorable W. Jeanne Meurer, Travis County Judge, 98th Judicial Civil District Court 854-9318	Here comes the Judge! Talk with the person behind the gavel. Learn how she helps kids who have made mistakes make better choices.
November 12 www.oag.state.tx.us/ child/index.shtml	Texas State Attorney General's Office, Child Support Division, Michael Hayes 462-6218	Parenting Awareness work- shop, emphasizing the legal and financial responsibilities of parenthood.

Figure 10.4 The schedule of speakers and events for Law and Order and . . . You!

Figure 10.5 Teens learn from EMS workers how to administer first aid.

Teen Feedback

The kids seemed eager to attend each week and enthusiastic during the presentations. They loved the hands-on elements and what could be personalized to their own immediate experience—trying out the dummy Automated External Defibrillator, wearing the Fatal Vision goggles, and talking with Texas Youth Commission rehabilitation graduates about the food in jail.

Chapter 11

More Programs for Teens and Adults and Teens and Children

OVERVIEW

An intergenerational program at the library is the perfect setting to bring two or more generations together for a meaningful and enriching exchange. All generations have something valuable to share with one another and time spent together in a positive interaction will help break stereotypes. Grandparents—natural ones or adopted ones—can provide the needed unconditional acceptance and companionship that teens need. Many teens enjoy helping and teaching younger children. These programs are included to give teens opportunities to interact with younger and older generations.

BATTLE OF THE BARDS, BY DIANE TUCCILLO

During the month of January, teens and adults can submit entries to a poetry contest at Diane's library. Application forms for both teens and adult levels are made available online at the library's Web site. The poetry is judged during February, and in March the nine winners in the adult and teen categories are contacted. Three teen advisory group members serve as judges with the librarian for the teen category. Three teachers/college instructors and the librarian judge the adult category. The first-, second-, and third-place winners in each category win gift certificates of $75.00, $50.00, and $25.00 to Borders, and a beautiful journal goes to each Honorable Mention.

The winners are invited to read their poetry at a poetry coffeehouse program in April. The coffeehouse setting is decorated with flowers donated from a local flower shop and a microphone is set up for the emcee and readers. Refreshments are donated cookies.

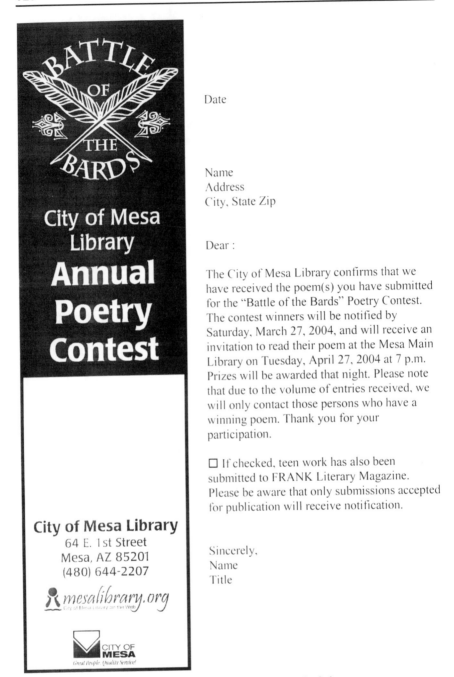

Date

Name
Address
City, State Zip

Dear :

The City of Mesa Library confirms that we
have received the poem(s) you have submitted
for the "Battle of the Bards" Poetry Contest.
The contest winners will be notified by
Saturday, March 27, 2004, and will receive an
invitation to read their poem at the Mesa Main
Library on Tuesday, April 27, 2004 at 7 p.m.
Prizes will be awarded that night. Please note
that due to the volume of entries received, we
will only contact those persons who have a
winning poem. Thank you for your
participation.

☐ If checked, teen work has also been
submitted to FRANK Literary Magazine.
Please be aware that only submissions accepted
for publication will receive notification.

Sincerely,
Name
Title

**Figure 11.1 The letter acknowledging
the receipt of the Battle of the Bards entries.**

March , 2003

Name
Address
City, AZ Zip

Dear ,

Congratulations! You are invited to read your poem, *"Name of Poem"*, at
the **BATTLE OF THE BARDS** Poetry Reading on Thursday, April 10,
2003.

The awards will be announced at the event and each participant must be
present to receive his or her prize. Additionally, we will hand out booklets
containing the winning poetry entries. Your family and friends are welcome
to attend!

Date: Thursday, April 10th 2003

Time: 7 – 8:30 p.m.

Place: City of Mesa Library
Youth Activity Room
64 E. 1st St., Mesa AZ 85201

Coffee drinks, punch and refreshments will be served.

Please call Diane Tuccillo at (480) 644-2735 to confirm your attendance.

Thank you for your participation! We look forward to seeing you!

Sincerely,

Diane Tuccillo
Librarian III/Young Adult Coordinator

**Figure 11.2 The invitation to participate in the poetry reading of the
Battle of the Bards.**

Collection Connection

Make poetry reading lists, and display poetry books and biographies of poets.

The Bottom Line

The expenses include decorations, refreshments, and prizes and had been over $1,000.00, but Diane halved the costs by asking for the flower and refreshment donations mentioned above.

Teen Feedback

The teens love this program!

BATTLE OF THE AGES, BY CATHY HOCHADEL

Make connections between generations with Battle of the Ages. Cathy pits the teens against the senior citizens for a Game Night, offering games that are popular with both generations. National Senior Citizens Month in May or Grandparents Day in September is a great time to schedule the competition.

Contact local senior centers, churches, and country clubs to find interested seniors. Borrow the games; you do not need to buy them. If you or your coworkers don't have games you can use, many places—senior centers, YMCAs, day-care centers, and churches—have board games you may be able to borrow.

Decide which games will be offered. Suggested games are Chess, Checkers, Chinese Checkers, Tic Tac Toe, jigsaw puzzles (two very similar 150–piece jigsaw puzzles), Backgammon, and Horseshoes and Croquet if an outside area is available. Set up the tables and games in stations around the library or in the meeting room. Explain to the players that there will be a set of rules at each game station, that the winner of each match will be responsible for notifying the scorekeeper of the win, and that the participants can play as many or as few games as they choose, but at the end of the gaming time, the contestant who is ahead in the game will take that win. Ask a volunteer or aide to be the scorekeeper in charge of the tally sheet.

The scoring for each of the suggested games is as follows:

- Chess: Match consists of one round of Chess.
- Checkers: Match consists of three rounds of Checkers.
- Chinese Checkers: This game may be played one-on-one or in teams (with an equal number of players from each generation). Match consists of one round of Chinese Checkers.
- Puzzle Playoff: This competition may be played one-on-one, but it is more fun to play with teams (with an equal number of players from each generation). Each generation is given a jigsaw puzzle to assemble; each should work at a separate table. There is no time limit, but the first team to completely assemble the puzzle gets the win.

GAME	SENIORS	TEENS
Checkers		
Chess		
Chinese Checkers		

Figure 11.3 A simple score sheet to tally Battle of the Ages winnings.

- Horseshoes: Match consists of one round of Horseshoes.
- Backgammon: Match consists of one round of Backgammon.
- Tic Tac Toe: Match consists of three rounds of Tic Tac Toe.
- Croquet: Match consists of one round of Croquet.

Fifteen minutes prior to the end of the program, determine the winning generation and present a winner's cup, medallion, or trophy. Display the trophy at the library until a rematch is held!

Collection Connection

Hoyle game rule manuals should be available during the competitions. Also display game software and other game and rule books from the collection.

The Bottom Line

Games can be borrowed to make your budget go further. Refreshments will be your main expense plus your trophy or medallions. Homemade trophies and donated refreshments will make this program nearly free!

BOOK BUDDIES, BY MARY ADAMOWSKI

Teens pair up with preschoolers ages four to five as Book Buddies for three 45-minute sessions during this one-day program. Book Buddies is an interactive way for teens to share their love of books and reading with younger children. Members of Teen, Inc, Mary's library's teen advisory council, enthusiastically agree to take part in the book buddies program. Permission slips and letters are sent to each Teen, Inc member and parent explaining the program and what the teen's role will be in the project.

The next step involves contacting the parents of the preschoolers who are enrolled in the current story time session. Letters and permission slips are distributed to storytime parents during storytime registration. Teens are paired randomly with the preschoolers. A second letter to the teens invites them to the library to select books that match up with the preschooler's reading in-

Figure 11.4 Book Buddies get involved in the story!

terests. The children's librarian presents popular and age-appropriate books for the teens to choose from, and gives them the first names, ages, and reading interests of their buddies. Tips are given to the teens about how to make their Book Buddies session a relaxing and pleasant experience.

Tips for Book Buddies:

- Preread the books a few times to become comfortable with the stories.
- Get acquainted with your reading buddy before you begin reading.
- Read slowly; do not race through the book.
- Ask questions about the story as you go along.
- Be calm if your buddy is distracted; try a puppet or puzzle.

The teens can take five or six books home to practice for their upcoming buddies session. Two days before the session, call the teens to remind them of the session and to ask if they have questions. The day before the event, decorate five reading areas, each with a different theme. Posters, puppets, and carpet squares can help decorate each area. Place additional books nearby in case the buddies have more reading time.

Follow the reading time with a cookies and milk snack. A local dairy and bakery donated cookies and milk for the event at Mary's library. The teens can give the children stickers and bookmarks. When they return the children to their parents, they can tell the parents about the stories and which ones their children enjoyed.

Collection Connection

Teens may like to share favorite books of their childhood, and the preschoolers are introduced to new books.

Teen Feedback

Kristi, age 13: "I love being with little kids and I love reading, and Book Buddies lets me do my favorite things!" Parents and teens appreciate and enjoy this program, and the teens ask to offer it more than once a year.

MOTHER/DAUGHTER BOOK CLUB, BY SUSAN G. BARHAN

Girls in the sixth, seventh, and eighth grades and their mothers met for about three hours to participate in a book discussion of *The Face on The Milk Carton* by Carolyn Cooney. Serve donuts, hot chocolate, tea, and coffee at the start and a pizza party for lunch. The refreshments are a good icebreaker and conversation facilitator. The mothers and daughters feel special when they come into a room with the tempting aroma of food and drinks. After lunch, create a collage to hang in the library that will generate interest and participation in this and other book discussions.

This particular age group was chosen because of the difficulties encountered in establishing and/or maintaining communication as peers begin to exert more and more influence. Mothers and daughters still need a way to communicate that is more neutral, less confrontational, and hopefully more nurturing than life sometimes offers in the bustle of everyday life. By discussing issues that come up in a book, parents and teens can communicate in a less threatening, less emotionally loaded, and less confrontational manner.

Share the responsibilities of presenting the author and offering a brief analysis of the story at future discussions. For the first meeting the librarian should present the information in order to provide a model. Each participant should have a notebook and a copy of each title. Access to hard-copy or database information on the author and critical analysis of the text is also important. It is also helpful to prepare a few questions in advance to get the discussion moving.

Collection Connection

Susan's library is establishing a Teen Collection, in transition from being called the YA Collection. These mothers and daughters will help that transition by passing the word along to other teens.

The Bottom Line

The first meeting was funded by The Indianapolis Foundation Library Fund. Refreshments can be donated or homemade and extra titles can be interlibrary loaned to save on expenses.

Teen Feedback

Two of the mothers in Susan's group have more than eight children each. One of them is even pregnant with her tenth child. Another one of the mothers has three daughters, one too young for the program and one too old for the program. All of the mothers have expressed gratitude over the opportunity to spend some quality time with their daughters.

The daughters were not able to express themselves with words as much as with actions. Now when they come in the library, they smile and speak to Susan. It is as if they realize now that they are important individuals in the life of the library. One daughter was asked what she gained from the experience; she said she had gained a chance to talk to her mother more about personal things.

Susan conducted a pre- and post-program survey. In the pre-survey she asked the mothers and daughters to list three adjectives to describe their family member. One daughter said her mother was "bossy, instructional, weird." In the post-survey the participants asked to list one new adjective that described their mother/daughter. The same daughter now wrote "grand."

One of the daughters from a large family said she gained "a discussion topic" from their participation. Considering what life can be like in a large family with all the hustle and bustle of keeping up with everyone, it was quite important that they had found a discussion topic that was unique to them.

One mother put it quite simply when she said that her "daughter appreciates the fact that I have cared enough to take an interest in doing something with just her." Her words really spoke for all the mothers when she said that now they are "able to relate to one another on a more personal level."

One of the mothers said that she was looking forward to the discussion because she and her daughter had "never done anything with just the two of them." She was hoping to gain some insight into her daughter's world, exactly the goal Susan was aiming for. She also described her daughter as "beautiful, smart, lonely" in the pre-survey. In the post survey she added "interesting." She also said that they had gained a new closeness and openness.

Feeling Safe

Tips for Teens and Parents

- Talk about making choices, violence prevention, safe communities

- Learn how to help yourself feel safe

- Enjoy pizza

Teens and their parents

welcome...come participate!

Monday, March 4, 6:30 to 8 p.m.

admission and dinner are free

North Liberty Community Center

Sponsored by the North Liberty Library and the Rape Victim Advocacy Program

Website Handouts provided by

Ambrosya Amlong, Medical Librarian, Mercy Hospital

Figure 11.5 The Feeling Safe promotional poster.

FEELING SAFE: TIPS FOR TEENS AND PARENTS, BY JENNIFER GARDNER

The Rape Victim Advocacy Program brought three representatives to talk with teens and parents about how to protect oneself from being a victim and how they can work together to make their community safe. They also discussed what teens can do to help themselves avoid being the victim of a violent crime. They spoke for about 45 minutes and answered questions from the audience. They also passed out information on RVAP, including free pencils and notepads. After they spoke, Jennifer served pizza and soft drinks to all.

Collection Connection

Make a display of informational materials in the room—books on date rape, victim's rights, etc. A handout of Web sites for teens on related issues will also be helpful.

The Bottom Line

Pizza is the only expense for this program.

Teen Feedback

The parents who came said the program was very informative and the audience was interested in the topics discussed. They thanked Jennifer for offering it.

POETRY CAFÉ, BY SHARON MACDONALD

For another twist on a poetry café, invite middle school students to create their own poetry in class and to share it at the library with their parents and other guests. This program gives the students an opportunity to read their own poems to an audience. Sharon set up the room as a café—with a microphone, tables adorned with red-and-white-checked cloths, and snacks and drinks served by TAB members. Sharon also hired a talented flutist to accompany the readers. The musician asked the students to give the mood of the poem and then she played softly as they read. When a reader finished, the audience would snap their fingers in appreciation. The TAB members who help set up and serve can read poetry as well.

Collection Connection

Some students may read from poetry books from the library collection. Display the YA poetry books around the room and on the café tables.

The Bottom Line

This program cost approximately $250.00, most of which covered the flutist, snacks, and drinks.

Teen Feedback

The students loved reading their own poems into a microphone. "That was fun, can I read another one?"

A CELEBRATION OF BLACK HISTORY, BY LIN FLORES

Lin's library coordinated a family celebration of Black History Month. She invited the African American Culture Club from a nearby high school to participate in a "Celebration of Black History" at the library. Lin contacted the club's advisor and explained the program idea. The advisor related this information to her students, who were in grades nine to twelve. They were very enthusiastic and 20 students participated in the program. The library's Teen Advisory Board was also invited to attend and participate. A microphone, a podium, and a CD player is needed. The African American Culture Club made their own flyers to distribute before the program.

The culture club members danced to African music, put on a fashion show displaying African dress, recited poetry, and sang songs to entertain an audience of 70. Refreshments were served and a good time was had by all. The superintendent, principal, assistant principal, school board members, teachers, and families with teens and children attended.

Collection Connection

Display books pertaining to black history such as prominent civil rights leaders, the Underground Railroad, Civil War heroes, and biographies with library pathfinders relating to black history.

The Bottom Line

The expenses totaled approximately $25.00 for cake, cookies, soda, and chips. The high school advisor brought refreshments as well. One of the local restaurant chains donated cookies.

Teen Feedback

Patrons said they really enjoyed the program. The African American Culture Club sent Lin a thank-you letter telling her how much they appreciated the opportunity to contribute to the program. The Teen Board member who participated said she loved it and had her father videotape the entire program.

DR. SEUSS DAY, BY LEAH DUCATO RUDOLPH

Twenty-five three to six year olds enjoyed celebrating Dr. Seuss Day, a program planned, promoted, and presented by teens in the teen advisory council at Leah's library. The program was offered on a Sunday afternoon for children and their parents or grandparents who cannot ordinarily attend weekday events.

The teens were assigned publicity, reading, craft help, refreshments, and

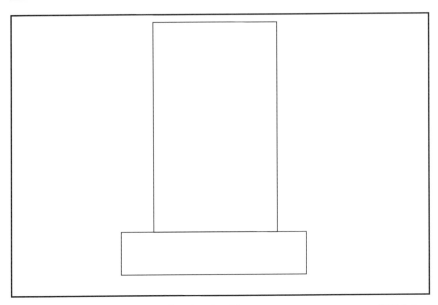

Figure 11.6 Enlarge the Cat in the Hat pattern to measure 8" high and 4" wide. Cut the brim 6" wide by 1" high.

cleanup during their regular meetings. One teen designed the flyer, which was posted throughout the library. Leah created a sign-up registration sheet that limited the number of participants to 25 and requested the names, ages, and phone numbers of the children. The sign-up sheet and flyers were displayed three weeks prior to the event. Leah made reminder phone calls two days before the event to those who signed up.

On the day of the event, ten teen volunteers arrived at the library to set up. They made lemonade, set up four areas for reading spots with selections of Dr. Seuss books, got the crafts ready, and distributed Cat in the Hat hats to wear. The Cat in the Hat hats were obtained from older teens who had used them in a jazz dance recital.

Two teens greeted the participants at the door and directed them to a reading group. There were four groups with two teens in each who took turns reading three to four Dr. Seuss books. Each group had approximately six children in it. Reading lasted for about one half hour.

When the groups were finished reading, the teens directed the children to three different craft tables and helped them assemble easy Dr. Seuss–related crafts. The crafts included a bookmark to decorate with a fish rubber stamp, paper Cat in the Hat hats, and Daisy Head Mayzie headbands created out of construction paper:

Figure 11.7 Teens helped 25 children create crafts, like the Daisy Head Mayzie headbands, for a Dr. Seuss–themed program.

- One Fish, Two Fish bookmarks: Provide fish-shaped rubber stamps, red and blue ink pads, and strips of paper precut wide enough for the stamp.
- Cat in the Hat hats: Cut two hat shapes of construction paper for each hat and glue together for extra body. Cut 12" strips of construction paper to staple to the brim of the hat on each side, measuring to fit the hat around each child's head. Cut strips of colored paper 4" long and 1" wide for the hat stripes.
- Daisy Head Mayzie headbands: cut strips of green construction paper about 14" long for the headbands. Cut strips of green construction paper about 4" long and 1/2" wide for the stems. Cut daisies out of white construction paper to glue to the stems.

Finally the children were directed to a refreshment table where they were served lemonade, Goldfish crackers, and Swedish fish.

Collection Connection

Dr. Seuss books were read at the program.

Figure 11.8 A Teen in a Hat shared favorite Dr. Seuss stories.

The Bottom Line

Craft materials came from the library and the refreshments were donated.

Teen Feedback

The teens had a terrific time and wanted to plan another event immediately.

SPOOKY NIGHT, BY MIRIAM PEREZ

The Teen Library Club constructed a spooky haunted mansion in the library to celebrate Halloween. They dressed up in their favorite costumes and told stories to children. A tent was put up on the patio and many, many garbage bags were used to create the rooms of the haunted mansion. The teens can decorate with Halloween decorations or make their own spooky displays. Four staff members used walkie-talkies to communicate throughout the library, to guide the children through the mansion.

Collection Connection

The teens and children look at the collection before and after the program. The program was helpful to make the community aware of the library and the activities if offers.

The Bottom Line

The expenses are about $100.00, most covering the pizza at the end of the program and the garbage bags for the haunted house.

Teen Feedback

Miriam suggests holding an open forum where the teens get to voice their opinion on the program. Record their ideas so you can keep things the same or change aspects that did not work out.

Chapter 12

Writing Programs

OVERVIEW

There is a story in all of us. Our lives, feelings, experiences, imaginations, families, and talents are unique to every soul on the planet. Writing is a way of sharing, connecting, and communicating all of these things with others. A blank sheet of paper can be an invitation or a barrier, depending upon the way our imaginations have been cultivated or stifled. Writing, next to reading, can be the most important tool for life success. Learning to communicate well through the written word assures a greater audience. Refining the work through editing and rewriting assures the message is what we mean to say.

Reluctant writers are not lazy or without imagination. They have had their thoughts, feelings, and ideas pushed back so many times they cannot seem to reach them anymore. These writing games and programs are tools to help young writers, even the reluctant ones, find their words, reach those ideas, imaginations, and experiences, and to put them on paper to connect with one another.

JOURNAL CLUB, BY DONNA CHILDS

The Journal Club is an informal group of teens that meets for an hour after school on Wednesdays to create writing and artwork. Donna purchased a supply of notebooks during the back-to-school sales. She collected old magazines, scissors, and glue sticks to make collages. She also collected a supply of markers, gel pens, glitter glue, stencils, rubber stamps, and hole punchers and sometimes brings in some of her own craft tools like scissors that cut fancy edges.

To publicize the program, flyers are handed out to teens and taken to schools. Signs are posted on the day of the event. The teens bring in friends, who then bring in other friends. The teens talk about it in school, because the first to arrive will tell Donna, "You're going to have a full house today."

On a typical day, snacks are set out—usually cider and cookies with a CD player and some art supplies. The teens don't have to sign up, and they can come to all meetings or just a few—the club does something different every week. Each teen receives a notebook, and if they forget to bring theirs, they can use a blank sheet of paper and paste it into their notebook later. Usually the first time they visit they want to decorate the cover, often with a collage of paper cut from magazines—words, phrases, or letters spelling out their name.

Just before they begin, Donna walks through the Teen Loft and tells the teens she has snacks downstairs. It has been a good way to get some shy kids or those not likely to join a group to become involved. It's very rare for a teen to come for just a snack—they usually want to join in when they see how much fun the others are having.

Donna makes up a handout of journal prompts, or she gives them other suggestions for projects. Journal prompts are just words or phrases to get you started in writing a journal entry. Some teens prefer very specific prompts, like fill-in-the-blanks, and others prefer open-ended suggestions. There are lots of books, Web sites, and magazine articles about journal writing, and Donna looks for ideas that can be adapted for teens. Donna also searches Web sites that suggest lesson plans for art teachers. The teens sometimes want to show the whole group what they've done, and sometimes they want to read a selection just to one other teen or just to Donna. Always ask first, out of respect for their privacy, if they want to share something with the rest of the group.

If the teens want to do something else, that's okay, too. One girl wanted to make a dream journal for her mother and one teen wanted to make Christmas cards. Overhearing a teen talking about her gym teacher's online journal, Donna said, "Now that sounds like a great title for a short story—'My Gym Teacher's Online Journal.'" "I'm inspired!" the teen said, promptly began to write a journal page in the voice of her gym teacher, and then read it out loud to the group. One of the boys made up wild collages of people using different heads and body parts of magazine pictures and gave them crazy titles. And somebody cut out words like "serenity" and "chaos" then drew pictures to illustrate the concepts.

Journal Club is a great way for Donna to get to know the teens a little better and to find out what's on their minds, and for them to learn about the library and what's important for their librarian.

Collection Connection

Pull books from the shelf that relate to what the club is doing that particular week. Some suggested titles include:

Capacchione, Lucia. *Creative Journal for Teens: Making Friends With Yourself.* Franklin Lakes, NJ: Career Press; 2ed.

Dahlstrom, Lorraine M. *Writing Down the Days: 365 Creative Journaling Ideas for Young People.* Minneapolis, MN: Free Spirit Publishing.

Gray, Alice. 2000. *Journal for a Teen's Heart.* Sisters, OR: Multonomah; Spiral Edition

McFarland, Evelyn and Saywell, James. 2001. *If—Questions for Teens.* Illustrations by James Saywell. 1ˢᵗ ed. New York: Villard.

Price, Dan. 1999. *How to Make a Journal of Your Life.* Berkeley, CA: Ten Speed Press.

Stock, Gregory. 1987. *Book of Questions.* New York: Workmen.

Vanzant, Iyania. 1999. *Don't Give it Away!: A Workbook of Self-awareness and Self-affirmation for Young Women.* New York, NY: Fireside (July 6).

Ward, Sabrina. 1999. *Spilling Open: the art of becoming yourself.* Novato, CA: New World Library.

Wilber, Jessica. 1996. *Totally Private & Personal: Journaling Ideas for Girls and Young Women.* Minneapolis, Minn: Free Spirit Publishing.

The Bottom Line

The expenses are minimal—most of the money goes toward the snacks. Use art supplies and tools already on hand for craft projects.

Teen Feedback

"I've been counting the days till Journal Club!"

THE WRITE STUFF, BY JENI VENKER WEIDENBENNER

A three-week series of programs, The Write Stuff, attracted fifth- through tenth-grade students to the library to learn how to focus on their prewriting strategies. Each one-hour-and-fifteen-minute meeting had the same framework:

- 3:30–3:45 p.m. gathering and opening discussion.
- 3:45–4:00 p.m. snack and group activity.
- 4:00–4:30 p.m. personal writing time (the program leader was available to conference with individual writers).
- 4:30–4:45 p.m. large group sharing time.

During session one, Jeni talked about how to think through a story's architecture (character, conflict, setting, tone, movement, etc.), and they did writing activities using magazines and a variety of dictionaries, thesauruses, and idiomatic-expression and slang guides.

During session two, they talked more about developing character, getting ideas for characters, and creating names. For the activity, the teens cut out pictures of people from magazines to create a character gallery. They wrote the name of their character on a piece of paper, drew circles around it, and in each circle wrote details about the character's personality.

During session three, they focused on setting up a conflict in a story and understanding how conflict makes a story interesting. For the activity, they worked in small groups to peer edit, share ideas, and collaborate on stories. They also completed personal writing contracts to set goals for the coming month and the current year.

A couple of packages of loose-leaf paper and a package of pens are the bare essentials, along with writing and literature resources from the library's collection. Jeni used writer's handbooks to cull ideas for discussions and activities, in particular Naomi Epel's *Observation Deck* and James V. Smith's *You Can Write a Novel*. She also referred to the Web site *Teen Ink* at www.teenink.com.

One special resource Jeni used was the Community Inquiry Laboratory Web site of the University of Illinois at Urbana-Champaign. Jeni created a virtual laboratory at www.inquiry.uiuc.edu/cil/index.php, accessible by password only to the teens in the group, so they can post writing samples, give and receive feedback, share writing tips, and ask questions. Using the lab is like creating a bulletin-board forum, with links to Inquiry Units (Web pages)—no html necessary!

In the future, Jeni plans to start each session by reading a paragraph from a popular novel and talking about the author's writing style and techniques. You can do this program with whatever writing materials and good books your library has on hand.

Collection Connection

The group focused on the use of dictionaries, thesauruses, and other language tools to spice up vocabularies and give writers ideas, but they also used research tools like encyclopedias and almanacs and periodicals to spark ideas for writing.

The Bottom Line

The only expense was for snacks, and parent donations kept the participants supplied with individually wrapped, nonperishable snack items.

Personal Writing Contract for:

My top writing goals for the month of February:

1.

2.

3.

I will accomplish these goals by doing the following:

1.

2.

3.

My top writing goals for this year:

1.

2.

3.

I will accomplish these goals by doing the following:

1.

2.

3.

Signed:

Date:

Figure 12.1 A personal writing contract for teen writers.

Teen Feedback

The teens were eager to continue the program, so Jeni scheduled a follow-up program for all the Wednesdays in March.

YOUNG WRITERS GROUP, BY SUSANNA HOLSTEIN

The Young Writers Group meets once a month for creative writing based on the writing prompts Susanna provides. The first meetings began with a workshop conducted by a local author and poet. She led the group through creative writing exercises to write poems, and left Susanna enough material for the next two meetings. Kids ages eight to seventeen were involved so the group divided by age after the first year. The older kids in the group now meet with a retired English teacher who works with them on writing longer fiction. Susanna found ideas for prompts in several books in the library's collection. Local authors and local newspaper writers have been guest speakers from time to time to give the teens a sense of the variety of writing careers available.

The group's writings are compiled at the end of each year and the PR department publishes them in a booklet complete with color graphics. Susanna organizes an author signing party and reception where the attendees each get a copy of the booklet and the writers autograph them. A local author was there to give a talk, and the teen puppetry troupe put on a puppet show based on one of her books. Other years the group has sold their work at a book festival. Many teachers bought copies as an idea to use in their classroom.

All that is needed is pencils and paper, and a lot of good ideas for writing prompts. You may want to give the writers folders to keep their work in. There are many books that supply writing prompts if the librarian can't think of any; also many good Web sites provide all sorts of useful information, activities, and exercises.

Collection Connection

Display books and videos at each meeting, and talk about them after the program. Use the books to give examples of specific kinds of poetry, to provide writing prompts, etc. Also show the teens books like *The Writers Market*. Give them information on local and regional writing competitions.

The Bottom Line

Pencils, folders, and paper were donated or purchased with petty cash. Guest presenters were free for the most part, although Susanna did pay the first speaker $100.00, well below her usual fee. The workshop fee was donated by a local utility.

Teen Feedback

Susanna started this program because a young patron, Rachel, usually very quiet and shy, begged her to do it. "Please, please, please, Susanna, start a writing group for kids!"

ANNUAL YOUTH POETRY CONTEST, BY AIESHA COLLINS

The Annual Youth Poetry Contest for poets in grades three through twelve runs through the whole month of April. The students submit one poem in one of four categories:

- Grades 3–5
- Grades 6–8
- Grades 9–12
- Poetry about Ohio

Librarians are the judges for the contest and they choose three winners and five honorable mentions in each category. Winners are notified by phone.

All participating students are invited to a Poetry Café in May. The café atmosphere was created with checkered tablecloths, candle centerpieces, and paper tableware. Individual cappuccino, hot chocolate, tea, and coffee packets are accompanied by baked goods contributed by the library staff. The winners are announced and they read their poems and receive their prizes. An open reading follows. All of the poetry submitted for the contest is published in a booklet that is distributed at the café.

Collection Connection

Poetry books are displayed in the library during the month of the contest and also at the café.

The Bottom Line

The expenses totaled $400.00 for prizes and drinks.

Teen Feedback

Parents comment on what a nice thing the library is doing for the teens. Parents and teachers support the program and teens look forward to it each year.

Entry Rules

1. Winners will be chosen in the following categories
     a. Grades 3-5 (elementary school)
     b. Grades 6-8 (Middle School)
     c. Grades 9-12 (High School)
Honorable Mentions and other prizes will be awarded in each category.
In honor of Ohio's Bicentennial, a special prize will be awarded to the students
with the best poems about Ohio.
2. Each student may submit one original poem that is no longer than 32 lines.
Please double check spelling and punctuation before submitting your work. All
poems must be printed neatly or typed. Make sure it is legible.
3. A committee of library employees will determine the winners.
4. If you are under the age of 16, be sure your parent or guardian is aware of
your entering this contest and is in agreement with all of the rules.
5. Poems may be submitted to the main library, the bookmobiles or any of the
nine branches.

If submitting by mail, send to:	If submitting by e-mail, send to:
Stark County District Library	acollins@starklibrary.org
715 Market Ave. North	Subject: Poetry Contest
Canton, OH 44702	(include the information on the entry
Attn: Teen Services/Poetry Contest	form below)

6. Poems entered may be considered for publication. By entering your poem,
you give your permission to publish your poem in book form or on the Internet.
7. Winners will be contacted by phone on Saturday May 10, 200_.
8. On May 17, 2000_ (5:30 pm – 7:00 pm) there will be a Poetry Café at the
Stark County District Library. Students may read their poetry and enjoy
refreshments. Books featuring all of the poems submitted will be available at that
time.
9. Attach the completed entry form below to your poem before submitting it for
the contest.

Entry Form
Please Print
Name: _____Phone# _____
Grade: _____ School: _____
Title of Poem: _____
I would like my poem considered in the Ohio's Finest category ☐

Figure 12.2 Rules and entry form for the Youth Poetry Contest.

Teen Journalism Boot Camp

Young People's Press
staffers and guest journalists offer you a journalist's
basic toolkit of skills such as interviewing, research,
fair reporting, and eye-catching writing.

Over four classes, you will complete a publishable
feature article, editorial or profile.

Young People's Press will publish your story on YPP.net
and circulate it on their newswire to
major newspapers across the country!

You will receive a certificate of completion to be used on
resumés and journalism school applications.

4 session series - July 14, 16, 21 and 23
2:00 p.m. – 3:30 p.m.
North York Central Library –Room 2
Ages 14-17 years

FREE

Limited space – register today!
Gateway Services desk or call 416-395-5674

Check out www.ypp.net for more information about Young People's Press

Toronto Reference Library
789 Yonge St. Toronto ON M4W 2G8
416-395-5577

Fig. 12.3 The promotional flyer for the Teen Journalism Boot Camp

TEEN JOURNALISM BOOT CAMP, BY SHARON MOYNES

The Young People's Press and the Toronto Public Library partnered to offer three four-session Teen Journalism Boot Camp series that were filled to capacity. Young People's Press staffers and guest journalists offered teens a basic toolkit of skills such as interviewing, research, fair reporting, and eye-catching writing. Young People's Press is a nonprofit national news service for youth, working to increase media literacy and show teens that it is very possible for them to get published. YPP helps teens find a story idea, encourages them to tackle the challenge of writing their story, and then sticks with them through the sometimes tricky process of publication.

To date, nine participants have completed a publishable feature article and Mandy White's story about living with cancer in the family has already been published on YPP.net. Participants are paid for published stories, a great incentive to complete a summer writing project.

Among the topics chosen by the teens who attended the TPL workshops were Feminism and the Younger Generation, Violent Video Games, Protesting through Music, Traveling in China, The Sitar and Youth, Hip-hop Fashions and Stereotypes, and Maintenance and Schools.

Teen Feedback

"Thanks for taking the time to do this for us. I was thinking about writing for a while. This workshop made me actually start writing. Hopefully I'll do that in the future." "I would recommend this workshop to my friends who are interested in journalism or writing." "The most useful component of the workshop was the guests. They were really cool and it was interesting listening to them." "Just a big thanks to you for teaching me for those four sessions. I had a great time and learned a lot about journalism. Hey you never know—maybe one day I'll be a journalist working with you." "The guest speakers were really helpful. They had interesting insights and were really outgoing people with lots of experience." "I loved the program but I wish there could have been more classes." "It was great. I wish it would continue through the school year as an extra push and to get us thinking."

Chapter 13

Teens in the Spotlight

OVERVIEW

The spotlight is on teens in this collection of programs. Teens share their experiences, talents, and creativity as they step onto center stage. Working with teens to help them put together a performance program creates opportunities to begin building nearly all of the 40 developmental assets!

OAKLAND TEENS MAKE A GLOBAL IMPACT!, BY ANTHONY BERNIER

In the spring of 2003, Anthony read a brief newspaper article detailing the plans of a local community service organization, the Lau Family Community Development, Inc., and their goal to send eight Oakland high school youth, ages 15 to 18, to travel to the Southeast Asian countries of their parents' birth. While there, the youth would not only study those countries and sightsee, but perform a variety of community service roles as well, such as to set up a computer learning center at a nonprofit organization in Thailand. It would be the first time any of the youth had traveled even outside of California.

Anthony invited the Lau Family youth to the library upon their return and enlisted the Youth Leadership Council to serve as hosts and emcees for a panel presentation featuring the teen travelers. The goal was to offer the youth a forum in which to share their insights and experiences with the larger community.

In every way, this event placed Oakland youth in the city's limelight—developing their critical thinking about the trip, providing a platform from which to share their ideas, practicing public speaking, and helping them and the audience value the library as an institution capable of bringing immigrant experience and history to the center of public attention.

The event was announced in local newspapers, flyers were distributed through the branch libraries and at the main library, as well as among the staff at the Lau Family Community Development Center and their participating youth. The most important and successful result of this program's promotion, however, was that the panelists' friends and family members constituted most of the audience. Eighty-five people attended the two-hour program held on a Saturday afternoon.

Youth Leadership Council (YLC) members served as hosts by handing out the programs they had designed themselves, setting up and breaking down the auditorium, and ushering audience members to their seats. A YLC member officially welcomed the six participating panelists and audience members, and introduced the adult project director of the Lau Family Community Development, Inc. The project director provided a broad outline of their project to take eight Lau youth back to the countries from which their parents had immigrated: Laos, Cambodia, and Thailand. A YLC member then introduced both City Librarian Carmen Martinez and Oakland Mayor Jerry Brown who officially welcomed the youth back to Oakland from their month abroad.

A YLC member introduced each panelist individually, adding a few biographical details such as age, school, and the country from which their parents had immigrated. Each member of the panel shared ten minutes of comments, details, and insights about the trip experience. After the panelists spoke, the audience took a ten-minute stretch and snack break. Following the break, a YLC member lead a 20-minute question-and-answer period with the panelists. Another YLC member took photographs throughout the event.

There are teens in your communities who were exchange students or have taken vacations overseas. Give them opportunities to share their experiences at the library. Photos shown on a PowerPoint program, artifacts and souvenirs from the trips, and any personal experiences coping with language and cultural differences would be very interesting to the community. My older daughter had the unique opportunity to travel to Africa when she was a junior in high school. She went on a safari in Tanzania. When she came back, she was invited to speak for several organizations. Sharing her travels with others reinforced her memories and gave her valuable public speaking experience.

Collection Connection

Display travel guides, travel videos, language tapes, cookbooks, and geography books on the countries discussed during the program.

**Figure 13.1 Promotional poster for
Oakland Teens Make a Global Impact.**

The Bottom Line

The only expense was the snacks, paid for from the Teen Services Department's program budget.

Teen Feedback

This was the first public speaking experience for all six members of the panel. Most of their post-event comments concentrated on how nervous they had been before the event: loss of sleep the night before, inability to eat breakfast that morning, uncertainty about what clothes to wear. One young man debated whether to wear clothing he had purchased in Cambodia, to wear a necktie and jacket, or to dress in his "regular" clothes. He eventually opted for the everyday clothes because he did not wish to appear as though he were "fronting" or representing something he was not. There were also expressions of great relief and elation after the event: lots of hugging and clasping of hands for having endured the pressure of public speaking and being "put on the spot" during the question-and-answer period.

READING RAPS, BY JENNIFER SINGELL-THANASIU

Three popular DJs judged this one-hour-long teen rap competition. Flyers with the rules for the contest were made and sent to radio stations, newspapers, and TV stations. Posters were also placed at all high school and middle schools, as well as at Boys and Girls Clubs, local YMCAs and after-school programs citywide. Students were required to register for the program. Library staff called to remind the teens about the event two days prior to the program.

When the participants arrive, they write their names on small slips of paper and drop them into a baseball cap. The librarian acts as emcee and welcomes the participants and audience and introduces the judges. The program proceeds in this order:

- Draw three names for the first three performers.
- Present a commercial break of two short booktalks.
- Draw three more names for three more rap performances.
- Present another commercial break about new books and sound recordings.
- Draw five final names for five more rap performances.
- Provide a ten-minute break for refreshments while judges confer.
- Announce winner.

The library staff was stunned by the quality of the raps produced. Some are so good that the library is considering using them in library commercials.

THE Chattahoochee Valley Regional
LIBRARY
S Y S T E M

Teen Reading Raps Contest
Official Contest Rules

Reading Raps will be judged in three categories
Originality
Presentation
Content

+ Raps must be written about the importance or significance of books, reading, or libraries.
+ NO Profanity or offensive language is permitted.
+ Raps can be no longer than three (3) minutes.
+ Teens <u>must</u> be registered in order to participate.
+ Participants must be present at the start of the program in order to to be eligible to perform. Numbers will be drawn out of a hat to determine order of performance.
+ Teens should bring four copies of their poetry raps' lyrics. These copies will be submitted to the library and will be given to judges. Please make certain your name and contact information is on each copy.
+ Winning raps cannot be altered in terms of musical or lyrical content between the day of the program and the day of the winners' recording session.
+ Participants who wish to use music to accompany their rap may do so. However, all music must be original compositions, and may not be downloaded or in violation of current copyright law.

Failure to comply will any of the above rules may result in disqualification.

For additional information, please contact Jennifer Thanasiu, Young Adult Coordinator or Wanda Edwards, Programming Coordinator, at 649-0780.

Figure 13.2 The official rules for the Reading Raps contest.

Collection Connection

Short booktalks and new book commercials were presented between rap performances. All branch libraries ordered additional materials on hip-hop, urban, and rap music, as well as how to write lyrics and how to freestyle.

The Bottom Line

The total cost of the program was underwritten by the Friends of Libraries. A local production studio covered the cost of the studio time. The studio was given billing on all publicity.

TEEN TALENT SHOW, BY NICOLAS BROWN

Teens can share their talents with friends, family, and the community in a talent show at the library. Nicolas, the president of his Teen Advisory Council, acted as the emcee for this program held after the summer reading program. The program was publicized with flyers and an electronic board in front of the library. The flyer was also enlarged to poster size and hung in the library. Teens register ahead of time to perform so the program can be planned effectively. An open stage at the end of the scheduled performances can give audience members a chance to share their talents, too.

After the emcee introduces the program and talks about the Teen Advisory Council, the first performance can be introduced. After the performance, the emcee can promote library collections, tell jokes, or talk to the audience as the next act prepares. Continue through the scheduled acts, taking a break in the middle of the program if there are many performances. Nicolas's talent show had about 50 people in the audience and five scheduled acts. Several spontaneous acts from audience members followed. Nicolas awarded the performers with candy.

A room with a stage and sound system works well for a performance program like this. If your library doesn't have adequate facilities, consider partnering with a local theatre or school.

The Collection Connection

Since this program was emceed by the Teen Advisory Council President, it was a great opportunity to promote the group's activities. Mini-commercials for library collections, upcoming programs, and booktalks can fill the changing time between performances.

The Bottom Line

Besides the publicity, the only expense was the candy for the performers. If the program is very long, light refreshments could be served.

Teen Feedback

It was a very fun afternoon for all in attendance and for those who performed. The teens enjoyed the program so much that another talent show is being scheduled.

LIBRARY SONGSTERS, BY IRA LAX

The Ann Arbor District Library, with support from Mervyn's, arranged seven three-day music residencies in secondary classrooms. For each one, a musician was matched with a social studies teacher to involve students in learning how traditional forms of music and dance reflect the civic, cultural, historic, and geographic themes that they were studying. Five hundred and fifty-five students participated. The themes presented include:

• Late Nineteenth-century Industrial Workers
• Civil Protest in the 1960s
• Music and Dance of the Balkans
• Songs of Latin America
• The Depression and the Blues
• Woody Guthrie and Protest Songs
• Dances of India

Two of the three days are spent in the classroom, with the first day devoted to hearing the musician talk about and perform the songs related to the theme. On the second day, the students learn how to write their own songs, play a traditional tune, and/or do a folk dance. The students supply most of the musical instruments needed, but sometimes the musicians bring a few unusual ones—washboards, kazoos, African drums, washtub bass, limberjacks, and other rhythm instruments.

All classes come to the library on the second or third day for a scavenger hunt, to do research on their theme, or to perform their songs and dances. Students who do not have library cards will receive them and a librarian will give them helpful tips on how to get the most from the online catalogue. Some groups do an additional skit activity, in which they research, write, and perform their own skits or TV news shows related to their theme of study. Ira, the coordinator of the program at the library, enjoys working with the teachers as they find new ways to integrate traditional music and dance into their classrooms.

One of the best outcomes of this program occurs when students who have not had much success in school become excited about the opportunity to use the performing arts to demonstrate what they know. It's a wonderful way for students to discover new reasons to use the Ann Arbor District Library, a great chance for Mervyn's to reach out to kids, and an excellent chance for the schools to further connect with the community. More information about the program is available at www.si.umich.edu/CHICO/folkandblues/main.htm.

At the end of the school year, Ira asks a few of the Library Songsters students to sing their songs at the free Summer Reading Kick-Off at The Ark,

Ann Arbor's famous folk-music venue. After the kids sing, a musician entertains the audience of young families, who sign up for Summer Reading and get a good show.

Collection Connection

The students who don't have library cards get them when they take the field trip to the library. The librarians go over the online catalogue and give them a half-hour scavenger hunt, which directs the teens to move all over the library to locate materials and write answers to questions. The goal is to familiarize them with the library and staff, with the hope that they will come back again and again!

The Bottom Line

Each three-day residency costs an average of $600.00 for the musician. The Friends group pays for the bus transportation from the school to the library. Ira has received funding through grants from Mervyn's, Ann Arbor Area Community Foundation, Rosebud Foundation, Harburg Foundation, and other sources over the years. The Ann Arbor District Library Community Relations Department programming budget supplements any needed funds.

Teen Feedback

"We liked creating songs, and at the same time we were writing our own history. When people look at what we wrote about they will think of 2001–2002. It was fun when San Slomovits came into class, and I learned about musicians from a long time ago." "It showed us how important songs are to America, how they bring us together." "I learned a lot about what circumstances the songs were written under and what they could mean." "It's so much fun to do research on songs, and it's so surprising to find many amazing facts about a time period that we hardly know about. It was also very fun to write our own songs; the feeling that you've actually finished a song by yourself is so great." "I have always believed in learning about America's rich culture and history, now more than ever. I really enjoyed learning these patriotic songs, which are important for all Americans to know." "This project helped me get a better understanding about the history of this country. I extremely enjoyed making the newscast; I wish we could do another set of songs." "It was a good opportunity for us because we got to interact with history." "One song that enriched me a lot was 'Deportees.' I found out how much people did to get into our country and how whenever an illegal was caught they were shipped back."

FROM THE TOP CLASSICAL MUSIC
SHOWCASE, BY LISA C. WEMETT

Inspired by the nationally broadcast public radio show from the New England Conservatory of Music in association with WGBH Radio Boston, Lisa thought the library could showcase local teens interested in classical music, as the local school music program is very high quality and competitive. Classical music fans of all ages enjoyed this one-and-a-half-hour program on a fall Sunday afternoon. When you plan your showcase, check with the school music faculty about scheduled performances for the school orchestras to avoid scheduling conflicts.

An auditorium or room large enough for an audience and a stage area is needed, as well as a room to use as a backstage area for musicians' instrument cases, coats, and tuning up. You will also have to provide music stands, armless chairs for performers, a small sound system for an emcee to interview soft-spoken performers, refreshments, and chairs for the audience and performers; an electric keyboard or piano would be great.

An application form was developed and distributed via e-mail to the music faculty, so interested students could get the applications at school, at the library, or off the library's Web page. Applications were due ten days before the showcase date. Applications required the title and composer of the performance pieces and signatures of the students' music teachers and parents/guardians.

Space was limited to 12 soloists or groups, with each performing for approximately five minutes, but Lisa says they could have accommodated 15 or more performances. Most performers played two selections. They needed to furnish their own music instruments. Although the library did not have a piano, one performer was able to bring her electric keyboard to play a piano solo. Lisa acted as emcee to introduce each soloist or group, using the format Christopher O'Riley uses on Public Radio International's "From the Top," a weekly radio series that showcases the nation's most exceptional pre-college age classical musicians. Each one hour program presents five young performers or ensembles whose stunning individual performances are combined with lively interviews, unique pre-produced segments, lighthearted sketches and musical games. A printed program gave the composer and titles of the pieces, and a short quote from the students, gleaned from their applications. Each application asked, "How did you become interested and involved in music?" "What's the best thing about playing music?"

At the conclusion of their performance, the students were interviewed with questions based on the application information: What other instruments do you play? Which is your favorite? How long has your quartet played together? Do other members of your family play music? From the one-page applica-

---

Application for "From the Top" Classical Music Showcase

The Webster Public Library is seeking young classical musicians to perform in the library's meeting room for their friends, family, and the general public on **Sunday, November 16, 2003, from 2 -3:30 p.m.** Space is limited. Soloists or ensembles may perform, with a solo piece lasting approximately **4** minutes and 6 minutes for ensembles. Ensembles should be no more than 6 performers; *only one application is necessary by one contact person for the ensemble.* **Applications and questions should be directed to Ms. Lisa Wemett, Teen Services Librarian, Webster Public Library, Webster Plaza, 980 Ridge Road, Webster NY 14580** (872-7075 ext. 111).

<u>Eligible students</u> There are no residency requirements. The student(s) may attend any school in the area, or be homeschooled; grade level 6-12; performance of classical music, either instrumental or vocal; must provide own instruments and music stand. A sound system or piano are **not** available. (Vocal performances will not need a microphone as the meeting room is not large enough to require it.) Auditions are not necessary. Enthusiasm and joy for classical music is a requirement!

Name_____
          First   Middle   Last   Date of Birth   Grade level
Address_____
        Street   City   State   Zip

Home telephone_____ Email address_____

Instrument (or vocal range)_____
I/We are applying as a: _____ Soloist _____ Ensemble
  Please print first and last name of ensemble members and instrument they play on the reverse of this form.

How long have you been playing this instrument?_____

Name of music instructor: _____Music school:_____

Academic school (p ublic/private/homeschool)_____

<u>Repertoire</u> (performance piece) should include a selection of no longer than 4 minutes for soloists and 6 minutes for ensembles. Cuttings and omissions of repeats are acceptable.

_____
Title   Composer   Length: minutes and seconds

Application for "From the Top" Classical Music Showcase (continued)

How did you become interested and involved in music? What other instruments and/or styles of music do you play? What's the best thing about playing music?

Once you have completed this application, please obtain these signatures:

_____

Print name of Music Teacher/Music Director   Signature   Date

_____

Print name of Parent/Guardian   Signature   Date

Please return application no later than Friday, November 7, 2003, at 6 p.m. All applicants will participate. (If performance spaces are filled, you will be notified.) Thank you for your interest!

**Figure 13.3 The application to perform in
the From the Top Classical Music Showcase.**

tion, there was a lot to work with from their responses, so the questions were varied and easy to develop. Unlike a formal recital, the goal was to let the audience see the performers as multifaceted—that classical music was just one aspect of these teens' busy lives!

A reception of punch and cookies was served for the students and the audience of around 60, which included family, friends, and the general public. Volunteer teens can hand out programs, usher audience members to their seats, act as interviewers, and serve refreshments.

Collection Connection

Display books on the history of classical music, biographies of composers, classical CDs, instrument and music books.

The Bottom Line

The punch and cookies cost $10.00.

Teen Feedback

At the close of the event, everyone was very effusive in their praise of the performers and the library sponsoring this opportunity to share teens' talents. "When will you do it again?" is always great to hear! A thank-you note was received from one performer: "I enjoyed playing for an audience outside of my school concerts. It was a wonderful opportunity to listen to other young classical musicians. It inspires me to hear such wonderful music."

Figure 13.4 A promotional poster for the Hip-hop Workshop.

HIP-HOP WORKSHOPS,
BY AUDREY LEVENTHAL AND CHRISTINE BORNE

The Progressive Arts Alliance, a collective of musicians, dancers, poets, emcees, visual artists, actors, and DJ/turntablists, offered four interactive workshops for teens at Audrey's library. Each of the two hour workshops focused
on one of the four elements of hip-hop: DJing, emceeing, break dancing,
and graffiti art.

Figure 13.5 Teens practiced break dancing during one of the Hip-hop Workshops.

The library provided flip charts, audiovisual equipment, power strips, and extension cords. The Progressive Arts Alliance brought a 6' by 9' piece of linoleum flooring and duct tape to create a floor for break dancing and custom music mixes. The Alliance required a signed parent release for each teen participant.

Collection Connection

The library created a handout for each participant. It included the categories *Read, Watch, Listen,* and *Visit*:
- *Read* featured books on hip-hop.
- *Watch* featured DVDs and videos.
- *Listen* featured audiobooks and CDs.
- *Visit* featured appropriate Web sites.

The Bottom Line

The workshops cost $1,000.00 for 12 to 16 teens.

Figure 13.6 The Teen Poetry Café promotional poster.

Teen Feedback

The teens wanted more! By the end of each workshop, each teen felt he or she had the skills to DJ, emcee, break dance, and create graffiti art. "Look at me! I am da bomb!"

TEEN POETRY CAFÉ, BY JODY MAPLES

A Teen Poetry Café celebrates National Poetry Month in April and Teen Read Week in October each year in Jody's library. A crowd of 80 to 90 teens attends each event. The Xtreme Teen Council sponsors the cafés, planning the decorations, refreshments, and publicity.

The stage is set with a black curtain and purple tube lights and the Teen Council bring their lava lamps, black lights, and revolving lights to give the room a cool coffeehouse atmosphere. Tables are covered with paper and a mug of markers for doodling. Poetry books are available at each table. Streamers hang in the doorway for the teens to pass through. Teens are invited to the jazzy café to read favorite poems and original poetry, or just to drop in and hang out. The students sign in when they arrive and their English teachers are notified so they might receive extra credit. Refreshments are self serve.

Musical performances and comedy acts are interspersed with the poetry readings. A guest musician plays guitar and sings during breaks. Create a poetry board made from a science-fair board to display with large Post-it notepads for teens to add poems. Display the board in the YA room after the program. The teen poets are encouraged to submit their poems to the Teen Council to have them bound in a book. Free copies of the poetry book are left in the YA room. Photos of the event are put on posters and sent to the schools for other students to see what they missed!

Collection Connection

Display YA poetry books in the YA room to help publicize the event. Booklists of recommended poetry titles are given to the English teachers.

The Bottom Line

Food is the major expense for a coffeehouse. Beverages are usually provided by the library, but ask local bakeries for donations of pastries.

Teen Feedback

The only complaints about this program come when it is time to go home! "I came to the Poetry Café in April. It was a wonderful experience for local teens to express themselves and feel understood while surrounded by their peers." Aimee Henkenberns, 9th grade

"What started out as just a little idea became a rather large success. I'm not a fan of poetry, but I had a blast and even made a couple of new friends. It wasn't just a night of poetry. We sang songs, read short stories, had all kinds of food, and generally just had a good time." Joshua Mouser, 12th grade, Teen Council Representative

Chapter 14

School and Life Skills

OVERVIEW

Teens can have a good time together learning valuable life skills and better learning skills in the programs described in this chapter. Many of these programs are perfect examples of libraries using their local resources, businesses, talents, schools, and agencies to present programs that are interesting and useful to teens.

TEEN INVESTMENT WEEK, BY VICKIE BEENE-BEAVERS

Teens can invest a week to learn how to invest their money. Coordinate a week-long series of 60- to 90-minute programs with local financial businesses and organizations, focusing on the different aspects and resources for investing each day. Vickie publicized the programs through newspapers, flyers, and the library's Web site.

The series of suggested programs included:

- Day 1: Federal Reserve Bank and the U.S. Department of Treasury
- Day 2: Local teen investor with National Association of Investors Corporation Youth Coordinator
- Day 3: Washington Mutual Bank and American Express Financial Services
- Day 4: Tour of Library Business Resources
- Day 5: Play Take $tock™ (or another financial-themed) board game

A bibliography handout can include a glossary of investment terms and a list of library resources. Add your library's investment magazines, databases, the *Wall Street Journal, Morningstar Report, Valueline,* and reference books with a brief annotation for each. Helpful Web sites to include are:

**Figure 14.1 Teens have some fun playing Taking $tock™
while learning about managing their money.**

- The All-New Teenanalyst.com. Available: www.teenanalyst.com.
- Sharebuilder. Available: www.sharebuilder.com.
- Tips for Kids. Available: www.tipsforkids.com.
- Young Investor. Available: www.younginvestor.com.
- Young Money. Available: www.youngmoney.com.

Collection Connection

Bamford, Janet. 2000. *Street Wise: A Guide for Teen Investors.* Princeton: Bloomberg Press.

Beroff, Art and T.R. Adams. 2000. *How to Be a Teenage Millionair.* Irvine, CA: Entrepreneur Press.

Burkett, Larry. 2000. *Money Matters for Teens.* Illustrated by Chris Kielesinski. Chicago: Moody Press, c1997.

Gardner, David and Tim, and Selena Maranjian. 2002. *The Motley Fool Investment Guide for Teens: 8 Steps to Having More Money than Your Parents Ever Dreamed of.* New York, NY: Fireside.

Kiyosaki, Robert. 2000. *Rich Dad, Poor Dad: What the Rich Teach Their Kids About Money—That the Poor and the Middle Class Do Not!* New York, NY: Warner Books.

Kiyosaki, Robert. 2000. *Rich Dad's Guide to Investing: What the Rich Kid In-*

vests in, That the Poor and the Middle Class Do Not! New York: NY: Warner Books.

Shelly, Susan. 2001. *Complete Idiot's Guide to Money for Teens.* Indianapolis, IN: Alpha Books.

The Bottom Line

The Take $tock™ board game cost $20.00. Snacks for the programs were donated.

Teen Feedback

The teens asked for more investment programs!

CLUB TECH, BY MELISSA PILLOT

A series of training sessions that build on each other will improve young teens' computer skills for home and school. The series of ten lessons, held once a week, is repeated three times a year at Melissa's library. An hour of guided activity is followed by a half hour of free time to explore. Design the lessons to build upon each other by introducing Word, Excel, and PowerPoint in the first week and then reinforcing that work the following weeks with projects utilizing their new skills. Also show teens how to better search the Internet for research and recreation.

The series of suggested lesson plans include:

- Keyboarding (Mavis Beacon software and Word)
- Create a Poster (Internet and Word)
- Write a Review (Internet and Word)
- Scavenger Hunt (Internet)
- Computer Music (Internet)
- Create a Web Page (Notepad)
- PowerPoint—Family Tree or All About Me (Internet and PowerPoint)
- Graphing with Excel (Excel)
- Word Search (Excel and Internet)
- A Party!

Give teens a disk at the beginning of Session 1. The students will add to previous projects on the disk to make a presentation at the end. The instructor keeps the disks until the last session when the teens can take them home with a printout of their work. Throw a party with snacks and music at the tenth session to wind up the series. Melissa invites teens to come to any session at any point in the ten weeks. There are typically five core kids and five to ten teens on a rotating basis, with a limit of 15.

Collection Connection

The lessons will help teens make better use of the software available on the library computers. For the "Write a Review" program, students may choose a book, CD, or movie from the library's collection to review.

The Bottom Line

Melissa purchases $10.00 of disks and spends $20.00 on snacks for each ten-week session. Since this is a repeated program, laminated posters were created with a blank area to write in the date for the next session, saving money on publicity.

Teen Feedback

Surveys are given following the final session to get feedback from the teens. Their favorite sessions have been Computer Music, Web page design, and PowerPoint.

FINALS CAFÉ, BY KAREN CRUZE

When the pressure of the semester finals builds up, teens need a place to chill out. Karen solved the problem of frustrated librarians and squirrelly teens during finals week by creating a Finals Café where high school teens could talk and eat and relax at the library. The café is open one hour each evening through the week before a final.

To create your own café, choose a room where the teens can make a little noise without disturbing the rest of the library. Hang posters on the walls that will appeal to teens. String white lights and light tubes around the room, and keep the overhead lights off. Set up a few card tables with chairs. Cover each table with a plastic table cloth or paper for doodling. Add a battery-operated light, some napkins, and a bowl of assorted goodies: lollipops, hard candy, and chewy candies. Play CDs from the library's collection, and display teen magazines and graphic novels. Place booklists and bookmarks out on a card table by the door for teens to pick up.

On a counter or a long table, arrange paper cups filled with a variety of Chex Mix and popcorn snacks, plates with cookies or brownies, and drinking cups with two-liter bottles of pop and individual small bottles of chilled water. Karen discovered individual bags of chips and cans of soda were expensive and disappeared too quickly.

When the room opens, teens can come and go as long as they aren't taking food and drink out into the library with them. Karen recommends that teens leave backpacks at the door, but books and notebooks can go in for studying. The atmosphere is more relaxed if a young person—a teen volun-

Figure 14.2 Promotional poster for the Finals Café.

teer or a college-age page, for example—is inside the room to replenish supplies and you sit outside the door to the room to greet the kids, tell passerby teens what's going on, and invite them in for free food and drink. At closing time, the bright lights come on and the music goes off. After everyone leaves, do a quick cleanup, and set up for the next night.

Karen promoted the Finals Café by sending lots of posters to the local high school. She also plastered the library with signs and put little folding cardboard "ad" signs on all the tables—in every department, on every floor. The event is also featured in the teen section of the bimonthly newsletter, on calendars and event notices within the Youth Services department, and on the library Web page.

Collection Connection

The booklists and featured collections of magazines and graphic novels are an opportunity to show teens some of the read-for-fun collections in the YA department.

The Bottom Line

Initial expenses were for lights, batteries, tablecloths, and posters. Continuing expenses are for food, drink, napkins, and cups. Karen spent about $79.00 for the three cafés, serving 60 teens.

Teen Feedback

Karen says most of the teens stop to say thank you. One girl hugged her because she thought it was so neat! One boy wanted to just stay where the music was to study. Karen notes that there has been a change in the behavior during finals week since the teens have a chance to chill out at the library.

CAREER NIGHT, BY BRIAN SIMONS

Choosing a career can seem in the distant future for many teens. You can inspire teens to think about their future careers and to begin setting goals to make them happen with a Career Night program. This one-and-a-half-hour program is also a chance for teens to meet people who have fun, interesting, and outrageous careers. While the teens may not enter the careers represented at Career Night, they will learn that no matter what profession they choose, even the really cool ones, there are preparations, requirements, and expectations.

The program requires four or five speakers who have cool jobs. Careers that are in fields of interest to teens are good choices. Brian invited a chef, a commercial photographer, a journalist, a skateboard-shop owner, and a barber who is also a punk rock musician and professional wrestler! Brian also served pizza at the beginning of the event. The wrestler and skateboard-shop owner were the greatest draws so they were the first and last presenters. All the presenters were local and did the program for free.

Figure 14.3 Who is the librarian and who is the wrestler?

Once everyone gets their pizza and settles in, introduce the first presenter. When that presenter is finished, introduce the next and so on. Each presenter spends about 15 to 20 minutes explaining what he or she does, how he or she got started in the field, how someone else can get started, mistakes he or she has made, job requirements, what he or she likes and dislikes about the career, and more. Ask the presenters to be informal, to take questions as they arise during their presentations, and to bring props or visuals if possible. Videos, posters, and equipment all capture the teens' attention. The wrestler let the teens try on his belt, which they really loved doing.

Brian notes that no matter which presenter was speaking at his Career Night, the same core elements kept coming up: schooling, training, networking, punctuality, professionalism, time management, and people skills. These elements were all driven home by each presenter regardless of the career type. Leave time at the end of the presentations for questions and mingling with the presenters.

Collection Connection

Display circulating and reference career-opportunity books at the program, including books about the careers represented at the program.

The Bottom Line

Brian spent $75.00 for pizza and sodas for 40 teens. The presenters were free. Remember to send thank-you notes to the presenters!

HOW TO GO TO COLLEGE FOR ALMOST FREE, BY SUZANNE DAVELUY AND EVA VOLIN

This one-and-a-half-hour program will get middle and high schoolers thinking about their college plans. The program focuses on four elements:

- Testing: Describe the college preparatory tests (SAT, PSAT, ACT) and show the library resources designed to help students study for the tests, including the College Board Web site at www.collegeboard.com.
- Choosing a College: Talk about state and private colleges in the area and local junior colleges, comparing tuition costs.
- Financial Aid: Define the various forms of financial aid: grants, scholarships, student loans, and work study. Show the FAFSA Web site at www.fafsa.ed.gov. Give specific information on tuition assistance at the local colleges and provide a list of questions students and their parents should ask when speaking with financial aid offices.
- Living Expenses: Discuss all the factors that go into preparing a college budget, including tuition, room and board, books, and transportation, and show a graph comparing the costs at the area colleges. The information can be found at the colleges' Web sites.

Follow the presentation with a question-and-answer period. Two presenters will hold the audience's attention better than one over the length of the program and can field the questions more easily. Juice and snacks can be served.

Collection Connection

Create a bibliography and display of library resources that help with the college-planning process: books and other materials on choosing a major, finding scholarships, writing essays, and living on your own.

Teen Feedback

Over 40 students and parents attended this program and the feedback was all positive. Most were surprised to see the many resources available at the library to assist in the college-planning process.

EMERGENCY!, BY AMY KORPIESKI

Young teens are often on their own at home or with their friends and need to know what to do in case of an emergency. Amy planned this two- or three-hour program to give teens some hands-on experience in basic first-aid response, home-alone safety, self-defense moves, and fire-extinguisher use.

Teens sign in and make name tags at the beginning of the program. Introduce the program and describe what you and the teens will be doing. Present booktalks on teen titles about emergencies—*Flight 116 is Down* or *Nature's Fury: Eyewitness Reports of Natural Disasters,* for example.

Invite a Red Cross representative to teach the check, call, care routine. Teens can experience hands on by practicing the routine with a "dummy" child.

Invite an officer from the police department to present an abbreviated form of a home-alone safety course they present in schools. The officer can focus on ways that adults may try to trick young people into opening the door, and he could also discuss weapons at school and the best way to walk away from a fight.

Invite a martial arts instructor to demonstrate basic ducks and ways to get out of a hold. He can get the teens moving by having them practice the moves. He may also focus on ways adults may try to trick young people—to get into a car, to come close to them, to put themselves in danger.

For the finale, invite a firefighter to introduce the students to a fire extinguisher. While still inside the meeting room, he should cover how to use one: PASS (point, aim, squeeze, spray). Everyone can then move to the parking lot where the firefighter can suit up and start a container fire. Every teen who wants to use the fire extinguisher can get a chance to try.

Amy said that, during the month prior to the program, their local fire-extinguisher provider saves any extinguishers needing to be recharged. This way they can let the teens discharge the extinguishers at no cost to the library. One staff member needs to be present for the whole program. Make sure you have a camera and take lots of photos!

The best publicity for this program is word of mouth—once you start talking with teens about fire and self-defense they will get excited. Talk to parents and teens in the library and invite them to the program.

Collection Connection

Open the program with booktalks about emergency and natural disaster books, both fiction and informational. Display the books in the YA area in the weeks before and after the program.

**Figure 14.4 A teen demonstrates that he has
learned how to use a fire extinguisher.**

The Bottom Line

The only expense is for small gifts for the presenters to thank them for their
time. Send thank-you notes the following week and include prints of photos
taken during the program.

Teen Feedback

Teens and parents love the program and look forward to it each year.

Figure 14.5 Which one is the self-defense instructor?

PIZZA AND POLITICIANS, BY JENNIFER GARNER

High school students can meet their local legislators and ask questions about the issues that concern teens at Pizza and Politicians. Jennifer issued formal written invitations to all the local politicians and then followed up with phone

The North Liberty Community Library presents a program for teens...

Pizza and Politicians

How is a campaign run?

What issues are important to our legislators?

When: Saturday, October 14, 2000
11 a.m. to 1 p.m.
Where: North Liberty Community Center
What: A chance to get to know your state legislators and ask questions PLUS free lunch.
Agenda: A teen panel will ask questions, and then everyone will have a chance to ask questions and visit more with the politicians during lunch.
Pizza and dessert will be served.

Why does someone choose to be a politician?

How do you contact your politicians if you have something to say?

Figure 14.6 Promotional flyer for Pizza and Politicians.

calls and e-mails. Jennifer advises that it is important to choose a time when the politicians aren't in legislative session and to give them plenty of lead time. A panel of four teens was selected to ask specific questions of the legislators about issues of their choosing.

Press releases to all area newspapers and to television and radio stations, as well as flyers throughout the community and at the high schools publicize the event. Political science and government teachers helped spread the word and offered extra credit to students who attended.

The teens asked questions regarding the politicians' views on politics, education, and other issues. After the panel's questions, the discussion was opened for questions from the audience. Many students came forward to ask questions and discuss issues. Jennifer had extra questions prewritten for members of the audience in case they ran out of questions but these weren't needed. Since there were plenty of questions from the audience to fill the entire hour of discussion, Jennifer believes that a formal panel may be unnecessary. This comment was also in the evaluations that the students filled out after the program. After the question-and-answer session, a pizza and fruit lunch was served and the politicians sat among the teens for informal conversation.

The Bottom Line

The pizza and refreshments are the only expense.

Teen Feedback

Jennifer received very positive feedback from the teens. The best feedback has been requests to do this program again from both a legislator and the teens.

TEENS ON CAMPUS CLUB, BY ELISE SHEPPARD

Elise is a Teen Librarian in a library that serves a community college and the public. The college has student clubs, and this gave her the idea of having a teen club on campus, too. She wrote a club constitution and submitted an application form for the Teens on Campus Club. Even though the teens were not college students, the college accepted the Teens on Campus Club as an official college club with use of the college facilities. The college is community oriented, especially reaching out to teens in the area.

Find out the rules for clubs if you want to start a similar club on campus. Elise needed to create an official structure for a club with a written constitution and officers. The club may need a sponsor and/or an advisor. The constitution for the Teens on Campus Club may be viewed at http://faculty. nhmccd.edu/elsheppard/constitution.htm.

Teens on Campus is an ongoing program. The Club elected officers at the first meeting, meets the first Sunday of every month at 4:00 p.m., and additional meetings are held to plan special events. The meetings are held in the library, with special events, such as sponsoring the Houston Symphony Orchestra or the Houston Grand Opera, held in appropriate venues on campus.

The club sponsors diverse activities such as monthly meetings, monthly movies, community-service activities, and music concerts. Two special-interest groups have evolved from club activities: Teen Poets and Teen Geocachers,

Figure 14.7 The Teens on Campus Club plans activities and programs for the community's teens.

high-tech scavenger hunters using GPS navigational devices. The poet and geocaching groups are conducted by college faculty members in English and Geography, respectively. View more of the clubs' activities at http://faculty.nhmccd.edu/elsheppard/activities.htm.

Collection Connection

Add materials to the teen collection that will appeal to the special-interest clubs.

The Bottom Line

Expenses include refreshments at every event, a library movie license, movie rentals when they are not available to borrow from the library, materials for projects, and the costs for performers for special programs. The library funds most of the programs.

Teen Feedback

The teens enjoy doing something fun, interesting, and social with their free time. They enjoy being part of the community college.

COLLEGE: WHAT IT'S REALLY LIKE, BY BRIAN SIMONS

This college-prep program is open to all high school students, but is most useful for the juniors and seniors. Schedule the program in late February or early March when colleges are closing registrations and going to college is on teens' minds. Invite an admissions officer and students from one or more nearby colleges to present the program. Ask them if they are willing to present a general-information program and not just a sales pitch for their own institution.

Advertise the program through program calendars; YA events brochures; signs and flyers posted at teen-frequented businesses; press releases to newspapers, cable television, and radio stations; Public Service Announcements on cable television and radio; and the library Web site. Brian also talked to various teachers and guidance counselors at the schools, and some of them gave extra credit if the student came to this program.

As the audience comes in for the one-and-a-half-hour program, offer pizza and soda and a sheet of questions to get people thinking. Once the participants settle in with their food, begin the program by introducing the presenters. The admissions officer and students can present an array of information—admission to an institution, what to expect from housing, coursework, homework load, time management, finances, the difference between college professors and high school teachers, campus life, choosing a major, and much more. The information may be presented in a lecture format and through audience-participation exercises and followed by a question-and-answer session. Wind up the program by informing the teens of the library materials available to help them prepare for college.

Collection Connection

Display books that assist in choosing schools, writing admissions letters, understanding financial aid, and gaining general knowledge about campus life.

The Bottom Line

Brian spent $75.00 to feed pizza and soda to 42 teens. The programs are funded by the Information and Adult Services programming budget. Additional funding was available from the Friends of the Library and the Library Foundation.

Teen Feedback

Many teens stayed after and thanked the university and college representatives.

1. How heavily is the ACT or SAT weighted in your determination of admissions to the School?
2. What other things do you look for?
3. Are recommendation letters useful?
4. What are you looking for in an entrance essay? Are you more focused on the content of the essay or the writing ability of the person writing the essay?
5. Is an interview necessary?

Figure 4.8 Questions to ask the admissions officer.

1. How are Professors different from Teachers?
2. How are the classes different from high school classes? Difficulty level, speed of material covered, freedom vs. responsibility. What is dorm life like?
3. Was there a big adjustment period because of being away from home and friends?
4. Do you need to know what you are going to school for right away?
5. Campus life, what's it like?
6. How do you know what classes to take? For a major, subject, Gen Eds.
7. Any tips on choosing classes? Word of mouth, Professor rep, etc.
8. What are the least and most homework loads you've encountered?
9. What are finals like? Multiple choice, or essay?
10. Do you need to own your own computer for college?
11. What's the longest research paper you've had to write?

Figure 4.9 Questions to ask the college students.

INTRODUCTION TO FENCING, BY LISA C. WEMETT

A cleared, open room with smooth flooring (rather than carpeting) is needed for a fencing lesson. Lisa invited a local fencing club to provide a one-hour introductory lesson. Two instructors demonstrated and gave hands-on lessons to 21 teens. One staff member checked students in as they arrived, observed the lesson as a "spotter," and took photos of the lesson. Otherwise, the instructors provided all content and supervision.

The whole group started together to learn some of the basic guard and parry positions and the terminology of the sport. The instructors then split the group in half. While one instructor explained the safety equipment and suited up the group to actually fence, the other instructor led the remaining teens in a variety of agility and strategy games. After 20 minutes, the groups changed places and the process was repeated. The instruction included basic

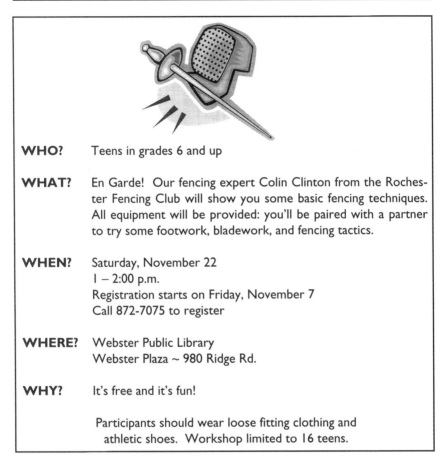

WHO?   Teens in grades 6 and up

WHAT?   En Garde! Our fencing expert Colin Clinton from the Roches-
                ter Fencing Club will show you some basic fencing techniques.
                All equipment will be provided: you'll be paired with a partner
                to try some footwork, bladework, and fencing tactics.

WHEN?   Saturday, November 22
                1 – 2:00 p.m.
                Registration starts on Friday, November 7
                Call 872-7075 to register

WHERE?   Webster Public Library
                Webster Plaza ~ 980 Ridge Rd.

WHY?   It's free and it's fun!

                Participants should wear loose fitting clothing and
                athletic shoes. Workshop limited to 16 teens.

Figure 14.10 Introduction to Fencing promotional flyer.

techniques: footwork, blade work, and fencing tactics. At the conclusion of
the program, the instructors talked to the teens and family members about
the club's programs and lessons and distributed literature about the fencing
center. The library needs to provide ice water and cups. Everyone gets thirsty
with all the exercise, and the suits and masks are hot!

The Bottom Line

The costs included $75.00 for one instructor and $30.00 for a second instructor, for a total of $105.00. All fencing equipment—jackets, masks, and
foil—was furnished by the fencing club.

Teen Feedback

Three days after registration opened Lisa only had three slots left in the class. Word-of-mouth publicity made this very popular with both boys and girls who recruited their friends to come!

THIS IS ME, BY CATHY HOCHADEL

A teen can learn what his personality type is, and find out how it determines his choices, affects his friends, and influences his future. This is Me is a program designed to make teens aware that the way we approach and react to everything in life is influenced by our personality. Learning about personality profiling helps teens perform and communicate better with others; and self-examination using a personality profile test allows teens to better understand themselves without fear of being judged by others.

Prior to the program find one or more personality tests that can be used by the teens. Copyright laws may apply, so plan far enough ahead to contact the author of the test. Allow time to read and thoroughly understand the personality types as described by the author. Books and Web sites with personality tests are listed in the Collection Connection for this program.

To begin the program, explain about personality types and why it is important to understand other people's personalities as well as your own; emphasize that the better you understand your own personality type and how you react to others, the more tolerant you are of other people and the easier it is to get along with them.

Stress the importance of giving truthful answers that describe who you are, not who you want to be. Remind them that there are no wrong answers; no one personality type is better than another. Explain various personality types as described by the test developer. Ask the teens to write down on a piece of paper the personality type or types that they feel describe themselves before taking the tests. Administer the tests to the teens. Then allow the teens to score their own tests according to the test developer's evaluations. Discuss their findings while refreshments are served.

Collection Connection

Display books on personality, friends, self-examination, or perception. These Web sites have personality tests:

Colorquiz.com. Available: www.colorquiz.com.
Colorwise. Available: www.colorwize.com/colorme.asp
Enneagram Institute. Available: www.enneagraminstitute.com.

Humanetrics: Jung Typology Test. Available: www.humanmetrics.com/cgi-win/JTypes1.htm.
Oxford Capacity Analysis Test. Available: www.scientology.org/oca.htm.
Personality Tests. Available: http://haleonline.com/psychtest.
Queendom.com. Available: www.queendom.com/tests.
Similarminds.com. Available: http://similarminds.com/test.html.
Tickle. Available: www.emode.com.

These books include personality tests and evaluations:

Birkman, Roger W. 1995. *True Colors*. Nashville: T. Nelson.
Branden, Nathaniel. 1993. *Art of Self-discovery*. New York: Bantam Books.
Godwin, Malcom. 2000. *Who Are You?: 101 Ways of Seeing Yourself*. New York: Penguin Books.
Hirsh, Sandra and Jean Kummerow. 1989. *LIFETypes*. New York: Warner Books.
Janda, Louis. 2001. *Psychologist's Book of Personality Tests: 24 Revealing Tests to Identify and Overcome Your Personal Barriers to a Better Life*. New York: Wiley.
Kincher, Jonni. 1990. *Psychology for Kids: 40 Fun Test that Help You Learn about Yourself*. Minneapolis: Free Spirit.
Littauer, Florence. 1992. *Personality Plus*. Grand Rapids, MI: F.H. Fevell.
Miller, Allen R. 2000. *Complete Idiot's Guide to Personality Profiles*. Indianapolis: Alpha Books.
Shaw, Tucker. 2001. *Who Do You Think You Are?: 12 Methods for Analyzing the True You*. New York: Alloybooks.

The Bottom Line

Expenses for this program include photocopies of the tests and refreshments, if served.

CAR REPAIR 101, BY CATHY HOCHADEL

"In an emergency . . . could you change a tire? If you start to hear loud knocking coming from the engine, do you know what to do? What should you do if steam comes rolling out from under the hood? Find out before you get your license!"

Contact a local garage or service and repair shop to invite a mechanic to present this program. Explain that you want the mechanic to show participants how to prevent car emergencies as well as to teach what to do when one occurs. Try to have at least two different cars available so that the mechanic can point out the differences and similarities between them. Be sure that the owner's manuals and keys are available and the cars are parked on a flat surface, not a hill. The mechanic should cover these areas:

- Fluid levels and how to check them and the consequences of neglect
- Tires, including air pressure, wear, and rotation
- How to change a tire safely, including the different ways spare tires can be stowed in a vehicle, the different kinds of jacks and jack placement, and the different ways hub caps may need to be removed
- Discuss best practices in common emergencies, e.g., overheating, dead battery, running out of gas, and low oil or oil pressure

This program should be done in late spring or early summer when many teens get their driver's licenses. Serve refreshments if desired.

Collection Connection

Display car repair manuals and, if your library offers ALL DATA, spend some of the program time in front of the computer to acquaint the participants with the database.

U-BUILD COMPUTERS, BY DANA BURTON

"Build a computer from second-hand parts. Grab your screw driver and let us show you how to meet the challenge: tear down and rebuild a set of computers in one hour. No experience necessary."

The U-build Computers program was created in 1999 by three high school sophomores who spent their spare time building computers from used parts. They continue to volunteer to be the primary instructors for this ever popular summer workshop. Two sessions of the U-build Computers workshops are offered each summer, one in the afternoon and one in the evening.

U-build Computers fits Dana's library's slogan for Teen Services, "stuff you never knew existed at your public library." It also fits their Teen Services mission: "to create programs and services by teens, for teens, on behalf of teens and in partnership with the community." U-build Computers attracts a largely male audience, incorporates peer facilitators/instructors, and literally costs nothing.

To create a similar program, Dana recommends taking the time to locate teens who can do the job, although arranging for an adult presenter would probably work as well. Your job is to host the program, advertise, handle room reservations and registration, and be their gopher. Request participants to register in advance and ask them to bring a #2 Phillips screwdriver. Plan for three to four teens per computer, plugged in and working, at each table. Twelve to twenty participants are a reasonable limit. The computers are used, discarded, and donated. The presenters can be responsible for gathering donations or can provide a list of acceptable components or models. The best deal is to get someone to accumulate and sort everything off-site.

If you don't want people playing with the computers before the program begins, try to maintain a "Yes atmosphere" by starting the program in another room and moving to the room with computers when you're ready for the hands-on part. Using a computer that everyone can see as an example, presenters talk the group through the process of disassembling the computers. Groups are encouraged to work together and to share the work. Presenters or other volunteer helpers are on hand to answer questions or help when asked. Presenters explain, demonstrate, comment, and advise throughout the process.

When everything is apart, the groups are given one hour to reassemble and test their computers. Presenters are available to help, advise, and answer questions. Over the years, the guys who presented the programs concluded that less explanation and more hands-on time works best. Since the computers are all used or discarded anyway, it doesn't matter if something doesn't work or gets broken. In fact, the most learning seems to happen when things break or someone doesn't get it right the first time and people have to do some problem solving.

During the last half hour of the program, the librarian highlights software, applications, networking, and certification books available in the library's collection. A "Finding Used Parts" discussion follows, focusing on using a local newspaper. Point out in detail how to navigate the classified ad section of the newspaper—a useful life skill and interesting critical thinking and literacy exercise. Also include a quick discussion of public property auctions: where and when to look for auction notices in the local newspapers. Wind up the program with a rubber chicken evaluation and a drawing for extraneous used parts.

For the evaluation, ask for a show of hands:

- Before today, how many people had added components or upgraded a computer?
- Before today, how many people had taken apart or rebuilt a computer?

Toss the chicken to a teen. When the rubber chicken comes your way:

- Name one new thing that you learned or discovered at today's workshop.
- Give one suggestion for the next workshop.

You may have extra parts at the end of the program. Participants are almost always interested in a drawing for the extras. As they respond to the evaluation, ask people to write their names on a piece of paper and toss them into a hat. Pull a name out of hat. The winner selects a used part that they want to take home. Continue drawing names until all parts are taken or no one wants another turn. There is no guarantee that the parts work, but that doesn't seem to matter! Extra parts are never mentioned in the program's publicity or during the program.

Collection Connection

Display and booktalk computer books, software, videos, and any other computer-related materials available in your library.

Teen Feedback

One year, a boy with no computer experience attended U-build Computers. A week after the program he came home from an auction with a truckload of used computer parts. He paid $35.00 for a pallet of miscellaneous computers and parts. He stuffed them in his bedroom, and over the course of the next two years built three working computers. Attending U-build Computers opened a door for him. It gave him permission to explore on his own. This program gave him enough confidence, information, and skills to throw himself into something unknown.

"U-build Computers is a great opportunity to finally find your way around inside that box on your desk. Teens learn how to construct working computers from used parts, or the newest pieces on the market with college students who have been doing it for years. You come away with not only the skills necessary to construct your own machines, but also the knowledge of where to find what you need to start." Levi Gray

"The students who have come to U-build are by and large not computer geeks. Many of the students know nothing about the inside of a computer. The experience of working within a student-instructor setting, even an informal one, has been extremely educational for me. Each year when we put together the U-build program it brings in a unique crowd of students, and I always learn something new. I feel that the experience of being able to help organize and run this program has allowed me to develop skills which will be very useful in the professional world." Victor Kinzer

Chapter 15

Teen Volunteer and Fund-raising Projects

OVERVIEW

Teens are great volunteers, if they are trained and appreciated and given worthwhile projects to do. Whether tackling a service project, fund-raising for an event or cause, or creating programs for others, a team of teens can make it fun with their natural creative energy and make shorter work of big projects. This chapter features a variety of fund-raising and volunteer projects that have been successful with teens in libraries.

Many libraries have had success organizing fund-raising projects with their teens, which can be especially helpful if your library says there are no funds for teen programming. While the teens are volunteering their time, fund-raising will take some organization, planning, and investment of your time. An ongoing fund-raising group needs to consult with an attorney to establish tax-exempt status, and many libraries will have policies concerning fund-raising. Friends of the Library groups traditionally fund-raise for libraries and are already set up with tax-exempt status and licenses, so they may be willing to oversee a Junior Friends group. Consult your administration before engaging in fund-raising activities with your teens to see what the policies are.

Unionized libraries also have policies concerning how volunteers may be utilized. Please be aware of what your library's policies are before discussing projects with your teens. There is nothing more disappointing than having a group of teens psyched up about a project, only to find out later they can't do it because of a rule you didn't know about!

DROP-IN HOMEWORK HELP, BY JOANNE RODE

Teens needing community-service hours and students ages six to seventeen needing help with homework can get paired at the library. This Homework Help program runs from November through May on Tuesdays and Wednesdays from 6 to 8 p.m. at Joanne's library.

Teens between the ages of 12 and 17 who are interested in becoming homework helpers fill out a volunteer application which is kept on file. All interested teens are accepted, and they can volunteer as little or as often as they like.

A log is kept in the children's room so teens can sign in each time they volunteer. They record their name and the date, the number of hours volunteered, the age of the student they are helping, and the name of the student's school. A calendar is kept in the log for helpers to sign up in advance. Teens are asked to bring their own homework in case there are not enough students. This is a drop-in service and teens are given service credit even if not enough students show up. In the first year of this program, 12 teens worked with 73 students for 88 1/2 hours.

Teen Feedback

"It's important to teach students how to learn and figure out problems in school and everyday life. It teaches them how to communicate with people and ask educated questions—in school and life." Andrea

HOMEWORK HELP CENTER,
BY JILL PATTERSON AND CARRIE ROBERTSON

Jill and Carrie's library also hosts a drop-in style homework-help program, inspired by a teen who wanted to assist elementary-aged students. They have over 30 high school students acting as tutors and homework helpers to over 40 students every day the library is open. After school, they help elementary school students on a drop-in basis. On weekends, tutors are scheduled one-on-one with the students. Recruiting for teen tutors is done word-of-mouth, and letters and flyers are sent to the local high schools—to counselors, Key Club, Future Teachers of America, club advisors, and English teachers.

All tutors go through a one-day training program led by the county's literacy coordinator and the library assistant who has professional tutoring experience. The training includes basic tutoring skills, reading skills, and awareness of learning differences. Tutors also meet one other time during the semester to discuss situations they have encountered, to encourage each other, and to learn a new skill for tutoring.

Your Library
Volunteer Application

Name _____ Date _____

Address _____

Phone _____ Age _____ Grade _____

Volunteer/ Work experience:

Special skills or interests:

Is your volunteer work required?   If yes, please explain:

Days and hours available:
__ Mon __ Tues __ Wed __ Thurs __ Fri __ Sat __ am/pm to __ am/pm
I would like to work _____ hours per week.

References:
Name
Relationship   Phone
Name
Relationship   Phone

Emergency contact:
Name
Relationship   Home Phone   Work Phone
Family Physician   Phone

Your Signature

**Figure 15.1 A volunteer application helps teens take the job more
seriously and practice applying for jobs.**

A teen homework captain acts as the coordinator of the program for the
day, checking in the tutors and students, ensuring that all the students are
getting help, calling for substitute tutors when one doesn't show up, and generally running the program so that the staff isn't tied up. The program builds
leadership skills among the teens and provides an opportunity for teens to
give meaningful service.

It is helpful, though not necessary, to have prizes for the students. Each
student can receive a sticker for attending a session and a pizza coupon after
earning seven stickers. Each student received a bag of school supplies and

candy at the last session in December. The tutors earn certificates at the end of the year and receive a little treat at Thanksgiving to thank them.

Jill and Carrie have seen this program benefit the teens and the students. The teens gain confidence trying new things and have learned to manage some pretty stressful situations by adapting and creating solutions. While the tutoring sessions can be stressful and sometimes tearful, the energy and time is rewarded by the results: a grinning boy coming in to say," I got an 'A' on my test!" and a girl who said with confidence, "I was able to do that hard part of the homework really fast later."

Collection Connection

Create a collection of books, flash cards, tutoring techniques workbooks, and other items for the tutors to use. Tutors and students are encouraged to use all the resources around them and regularly look up things in dictionaries, books on grammar, math, and science.

The Bottom Line

The main expense is for this program is for the refreshments for the tutor training session. Local businesses can donate school supplies and local restaurants provide pizza coupons to reward the students at the end of the semester.

Teen Feedback

The teens created and designed the program through the Teen Advisory Board. After the first semester, the teens met to evaluate the program and suggested changes and improvements, which were implemented. At the end of each semester, surveys are handed out to the parents, the tutors, and the students to receive input. One parent stated, "Yes, I sure did [find the Homework Help Center helpful]!!! My daughter understood the work, and when she brought home her first 100 percent on her math, it was the best moment for her and for myself." In response to "What was your favorite part of Homework Help?," her daughter wrote, "When I got an A+ on my math test from Mark helping me." Another parent said, "Their [her children's] test scores improved. My children enjoyed coming here and looked forward to doing their homework." In response to "What did you like most about tutoring?" teen tutors responded, "Being able to teach students and help them understand certain aspects of what they need to learn"; "The feeling like you're helping people"; "The kids were interesting, awesome little kids"; "Seeing the kids understand what they are being taught"; "Seeing kids try their best to learn." In response to "What did you learn (about yourself, others, tutoring—anything)?" teen tutors stated, "I learned that teaching and tutoring take a lot of time and patience"; "That I do enjoy helping the younger kids"; "I

Figure 15.2 The spring-cleaning crew shows the tools of the trade.

learned that it is not easy to get information into a kid's head; it takes patience"; "I learned that helping others can really be rewarding."

SPRING CLEANING @ THE LIBRARY, BY AMY KORPIESKI

The library gets a spring cleaning during spring break! Middle school students come to a morning, afternoon, or evening cleaning session and return on Friday for a one-hour pizza party and teen advisory board meeting. A maximum of 12 teens attend each session.

The students start as a group in the meeting room. They make nametags that include the word "volunTEEN" so everyone in the library knows that they are great volunteers. The students divide into teams of two and pick an area of the library from a hat. Amy explains how to dust a shelf of books to keep the books in order. Dust cloths with a dust-catching agent and gloves are available for students who want them. Students then find their section and start cleaning. The volunTEENs clean for an hour and a half.

The teens receive a "Thank you for volunTEENing" card that is an invitation to the pizza party. All of the cards have a sticker or stamp on the back and are used for drawing door prizes at the party. The pizzas are donated by local businesses. During the pizza snack they also hold a teen advisory board meeting.

Collection Connection

Having the students in the stacks exposes them to lots of books—and they always find new and interesting things to check out. Many students spend as much time browsing as they do dusting.

The Bottom Line

The dust cloths and gloves were provided as a regular part of the cleaning supplies. Large chains are usually willing to donate a pizza or two.

Teen Feedback

Teens loved volunteering and feeling useful to the library. Teens start asking about the annual event in January.

TEENS ONLINE, BY ANN MELROSE

Teens Online is a volunteer advisory board for the TeenLinks Web site at www.hclib.org/teens. Teens in grades eight through twelve can be a member of the technology-based group. Teens Online meets once a month on a Sun-

Figure 15.3 A great group of teens like this will get a lot of cleaning done in a very short time.

day afternoon from November through April at the library in a room equipped with a computer, an online connection, and a video projector and screen. Each Teens Online group represents the unique talents and interests of its participants, which typically vary from year to year. Group members work on Web-based projects on their own computers between meetings. Each Teens Online member needs a personal, active e-mail address and account. Four youth services teen librarians advise the group, with assistance from the public Web-page administrator and the graphics designer.

Teens Online volunteers work to:

- Develop and maintain Web pages for the Free Time section of TeenLinks.
- Write book, game, software, and/or music reviews.
- Review TeenLinks Web pages and suggest improvements.
- Suggest and review Web sites for TeenLinks.
- Offer advice on marketing TeenLinks.

Specific pages within TeenLinks created by Teens Online include:

- Free Time at www.hclib.org/teens/free.html A collection of links and articles.
- Homework Help: Internet Search Engines at www.hclib.org/teens/search_engines.cfm.

Figure 15.4 The Teens Online volunteers wear shirts displaying the TeenLinks graphics from the library's teen Web page.

- Read On: Teens Pick at www.hclib.org/teens/read_teens_pick.html Teens list their Top Ten Favorite Books.
- An annotated list of search engines.

A new group is formed each school year. The following steps are taken to recruit new Teens Online volunteers:

- Teens Online job description and online application are posted on the TeenLinks home page for six weeks, mid-August through September.
- Recruitment information is included in the Hennepin County Library public newsletter.
- Youth Services librarians encourage interested teen volunteers to apply.
- Area high school media specialists encourage interested teens to apply.
- The library Volunteer Coordinator screens and interviews (by phone and mail) teens who have applied.
- The Volunteer Coordinator and TeenLinks Coordinator together select the Teens Online advisory board.

Once Teens Online volunteers are selected, their contributions to the TeenLinks Web site are promoted on the TeenLinks home page. School media specialists are also notified when their students have joined and contributed to Teens Online. Occasionally, Teens Online activities are also promoted on the library's home page.

Collection Connection

Teens Online volunteers create a list of their own top ten favorite books for the TeenLinks —>Read On Web page. The teens create their lists online using the library catalog feature called My List.

The Bottom Line

Expenses average $10.00 per meeting for beverages and snacks, plus $30.00 for pizza once during the year, for a total of about $100.00 a year. Other expenses, such as prizes for a Web site contest sponsored by Teens Online, are also funded as needed.

Teen Feedback

"One of the best things about Teens Online is getting the opportunity to show Web sites I've designed to the many users who visit TeenLinks." "It is rare that a teen's work gets so much respect and recognition . . . . We are definitely still contributing to the community." "Few volunteer opportunities let teens directly contribute to a project and then allow them to see immediate results." "My additions and feedback are welcomed and utilized more than other opportunities I've had." "It is a unique opportunity because it pulls teens from all over the county, whereas many of the other opportunities I have had have been with teens from my school."

TEEN ADVISORY BOARD FIELD TRIP, BY MELISSA SILLITOE

Melissa created a great way to kick off a new Teen Advisory Board. She invited several teen patrons on a field trip to discuss forming a TAB. Parents signed permission slips and the group took a minivan trip to another branch. The teens explored the teen section, making notes on what they liked. Melissa and the teens then went to McDonalds and had a planning meeting, brainstorming about teen programs. They now meet monthly to plan programs and request materials to purchase for the collection.

READING BUDDIES, BY SHARON MOYNES

Sharon's library, like Mary Adamowski's Book Buddies program in Chapter 11, pairs up teens and children to read together. Sharon promotes the program as a project to fulfill volunteer requirements; the teens participate for seven weeks.

**TEEN VOLUNTEERS
NEEDED FOR READING BUDDIES PROGRAM
Summer 2003**

Do you love to work with children and have strong English language skills?

North York Central Library will be offering a summer program that pairs teen volunteers 14 to 18 years old with younger children to participate in fun reading based activities that reinforce the joy of reading.

Participants must pre-register by calling
416-395-5674 or 416-395-5784 on or before June 26th.

Participants must also attend a training session provided by Frontier College on Thursday, June 26th from 6:30 p.m. to 8:15 p.m.

Location: North York Central Library
Children's Storyroom, Main Floor

Teen volunteers will meet with their buddies for six Thursday afternoon sessions and attend a Thursday morning wrap up session with special guest author Cora Taylor on Wednesday, August 21.

Thursdays, July 10- August 14, 1:45 p.m.-3:15 p.m.
Thursday, August 21, 10:15 a.m.11:45 a.m.

Time counts for your high school Volunteer Hours requirement. Upon completion of the program, you will get a record of your volunteer service.

To register call 416-395-5674 or 416-395-5784
or send an email with name, age and telephone # to
smoynes@tpl.toronto.on.ca

North York Central Library THE HUB 5120 Yonge Street, North York, Ont., M2N 5N9

Figure 15.5 The Reading Buddies recruitment flyer.

PENNIES FOR AFRICA, BY LAURA CLEVELAND

Laura's library partnered with UNICEF to collect pennies to send to Africa. She began organizing the program through municipal channels since the collection would be in a city park, located behind the library. The local police department approved the UNICEF representative on record to be sure the

---

YOU CAN HELP TO MAKE A BETTER WORLD!

Teen Volunteers will be collecting your rolled pennies for
UNICEF
at the Capp Smith Park Pavilion (behind the library)
on Saturday, July 19th from 1-5 pm.

SEND HOPE from your children to the children of South Africa--
YOU CAN HELP TO MAKE A BETTER WORLD!

For more information: (817) 514-5866

Figure 15.6 A promotional flyer for Pennies for Africa.

library would be donating to a genuine charity, and then gave the program a go-ahead.

The program was promoted on half-sheet flyers given to teens attending the summer reading programs. Instead of going door-to-door to solicit money from strangers, teens were encouraged to spread the word to friends, neighbors, and church groups to save pennies for the event.

On the final afternoon of Summer Reading, the collection was taken up at the park in lots of plastic buckets. Twelve teen volunteers oversaw the penny collection and the Youth Librarian checked in frequently. Following an African story hour, teens rolled pennies and had a hamburger party. The group raised $341.50 in pennies for Africa!

Collection Connection

An African storyteller told stories the hour before the party began and Laura created a book display.

The Bottom Line

Laura spent about $40.00 for the hamburger party at the park.

Teen Feedback

Veronica G. said, "I thought it was a great idea! I felt like it really taught other children about the whole world. In the area where we live, we don't hear a lot about the different regions, but we got to think about how other kids live."

**Figure 15.7 Teens collected pennies and enjoyed
an afternoon of African stories and a cookout.**

Sarah L. said, "It was so hot outside [nearly 105 degrees] and I kept thinking . . . it's hotter in Africa and we have water and they don't!"

BABYSITTING, BY JENNIFER GARNER

During the weeks before the December holidays, the teens can raise funds by holding a shoppers' babysitting clinic. Libraries near shopping areas can take advantage of their location in the promotion for a babysitting program. Teens can read to their charges, play games with them, or watch movies with them.

Depending upon the number of teens and the facilities available, you may want to preregister to limit the ages and number of children you accept into the program. Consider also if you want babies in diapers or potty-trained toddlers, babies who need to be carried or only walkers. Set a limited time frame and a flat fee per child. Jennifer's group charged $10.00 for one child for the afternoon or $20.00 for more than one child for a five-hour time frame.

Each teen can be assigned three to four children. It is helpful to separate into groups of smaller kids and older kids so they can participate in different activities. Scheduled activities can keep the afternoon moving along smoothly. Jennifer advises to include a late fee on the registration: $10.00 for every 15 minutes late per child.

SHELV-X, BY LISA THARP

During a short-staffed and lean budget time, Lisa's library developed a huge backlog of books needing to be shelved. Despite everyone's best efforts, there were always in excess of 15 trucks left over at the end of the day and the shelves themselves were a shambles because there was no time for the usual shelf-reading. In an effort to get caught up, Lisa invented Shelv-X.

Teens were invited to the library for four hours on a Sunday morning when the library was closed to help put things in order. The teen council paid for donuts, bagels, and pop, and the teens brought their own radios. It was billed as a "get away from adults" type of event. Lisa and a teen page oversaw the program.

Lisa made Shelv-X coupons and put one on each shelf. The trucks of books to be shelved were presorted into their genres, J fiction, Adult Mysteries, teen nonfiction, etc., and the carts were rolled into their areas. The teens took an armload of books to shelve and went at it. Each time they found a Shelv-X coupon, they had the opportunity to shelf-read that shelf in order to keep the coupon. When the shelf was ready for inspection, the teen called a staff member to check his work. If everything was in order, allowing up to three books to be out of place, the teen was given the coupon to later redeem for prizes. A sticker was put on the shelf so the staff would know it had been shelf read. At the end of the morning, the teens used their accumulated coupons like money at an auction of prizes that had been donated by the staff or were part of Lisa's cache of cool giveaways. The teens loved bidding for the prizes.

Lisa promoted Shelv-X with posters in the library. Teens preregistered so Lisa knew who and how many to expect, especially since the library was closed during the event. When the teens signed in the morning of Shelv-X they were required to provide a contact in case of emergency.

Collection Connection

The teens become more familiar with how books are arranged in the library and got a chance to look over many titles.

The Bottom Line

The only expense was the food, which cost less than $20.00.

Teen Feedback

The teens thought it was very cool to have the library to themselves and to make a direct contribution. This program brought in a different crowd of teens. One boy brought his buddy and they had a great time discovering the mis-shelved books and just yakking away about whatever. The camaraderie reminded Lisa of watching guys work on cars or computers or painting houses. Several people commented that they'd enjoy coming back to do it again— even without the food.

STARTING A TEEN ADVISORY BOARD, BY LISA C. WEMETT

As part of a research project for course credit, a student intern from the library school at the University of Buffalo became the "resident expert" on teen advisory boards at Lisa's library. She researched what groups were doing around the country, how they started their groups, and ways to keep the group going. To locate members for the TAB, the intern administered a survey in the schools on library services and programs. The final question on the survey, distributed to a sample of 232 students in the local middle and high schools, was "Would you be interested in serving on a Teen Advisory Board? Yes/No/Tell me more."

The intern tabulated the surveys, which also included lines for the student's name, address, and telephone. A volunteer reviewed all the surveys that stated the student was interested in the advisory board or wanted to know more. The volunteer addressed envelopes to these teens and a mailing was developed with a letter of invitation and an application form. Of the 47 students invited to join the TAB, nine submitted applications and eight attended the first meeting in February 2003. The group now averages ten members per meeting.

The intern worked closely with the two Teen Services Librarians to consider what to include in the first two meeting agendas and also attended the first meeting. The intent from the beginning has been to directly involve teens in library decisions that affect their use of the library. Meeting activities included providing direct input into library collection purchases for music, fiction, graphic novels, and DVDs, especially anime. The group selected the 2003 summer-reading theme, reviewed program ideas, and voted on incentive prizes for the program.

Many of the program ideas that were collected from the services survey

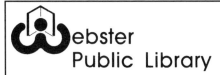 Public Library

Teen Services Department
Webster Plaza, 980 Ridge Road
Webster, New York 14580
(585) 872-7075 ext. 113 Olivia Durant
www.websterlibrary.org

Dear Webster Teen:

In November, you completed a survey on services at the Webster Public Library. You are receiving this letter because you expressed an interest in serving on a teen advisory board.

Webster Public Library believes that teens should have a say in issues that concern them at the library. A teen advisory board is being initiated to sound out the teen population in Webster. The board will meet once a month to help the Teen Services Department of the Webster Public Library in planning services, library programs, and collections for teens in Webster. Our first meeting will be in February 2003.

We encourage you to let your voice be heard and represent Webster teens in discussing what young adults would like for the library. If you (or someone you know) would like to share your opinions, enjoy monthly activities, and have fun, we hope you will apply. Applications from Webster residents in middle and high school are being accepted, with openings to represent each Webster school building. A form is enclosed for your convenience. We would like you to return it to us **by Monday, January 13, 2003**.

If you have questions about the Teen Advisory Board, please call me at 872-7075, ext. 113, or Ms. Lisa Wemett at ext. 111. Hope to hear from you!

Sincerely,

Olivia S. Durant
Teen Services Librarian

Figure 15.8 A letter of invitation to serve on the Teen Advisory Board.

were later ranked by the TAB. Popular activities for the TAB were a buying trip to a local chain bookstore in August to select books and music for the library's collections, a lock-in overnight in the library in December, and the selection of new furniture for the Teen Lounge.

Two staff members meet with the TAB for one hour each month. The advisors prepare for the meeting by collaborating on the meeting agenda, purchasing refreshments, preparing to lead activities at the meeting (e.g., surveys and icebreaker games), and brainstorming future projects to put forth

Let your voice be heard!

   Webster Public Library
Teen Advisory Board
Application

The Teen Library Advisory Board offers teens the opportunity to contribute ideas for planning library programs, services, and collections for teens in Webster. Participation is open to Webster residents in middle and high school. Board positions will be limited, with representatives from each school in Webster.

Name_____

Address_____
Telephone_____ E-mail_____
School _____ Grade (2003-2004)_____
Please list any sports and school activities you are involved in. Please indicate the number of years and your level of participation (e.g., team captain, class officer, committee chair, etc.).

Tell us why you would like to join the teen advisory board. Check all that apply:
____Help with programming
____Writing book reviews or discussing books
____Advising librarians about new purchases of books, videos, and CDs
____Give suggestions for improving the teen space at the library
____Decorating or making bulletin boards or displays
Other_____

What skills or personal qualities would you bring to the Teen Advisory Board? Here's your chance to tell us what you think. If you could change one thing at the Webster Public Library, what would you change? Please use the allotted space.

Currently, meetings are the second Thursday of the month, from 7:30-8:30. Are you able to attend regularly at this time? (circle one)   **YES   NO**

Student's signature_____
Parent or guardian's signature_____ Date_____
Please return completed application to:
  Olivia S. Durant, Teen Services Librarian
  Webster Public Library, Webster Plaza, 980 Ridge Road, Webster, NY 14580
  (585) 872-7075

Figure 15.9 A Teen Advisory Board application. Completing the form helps the teens think about their involvement and commitment.

to the group. One staff member e-mails reminders to the group members about the upcoming meeting date.

Collection Connection

At each meeting, TAB members may select from new fiction and nonfiction titles processed in the past four weeks. These books are put aside so they have first dibs on the new materials. Galley copies of forthcoming teen novels are loaned to interested members.

The Bottom Line

The expenses average $6.00 per month for refreshments, which is covered by the Friends of the Webster Public Library. To cut costs, students take turns bringing the refreshments and contributing a two-liter bottle of soda.

Teen Feedback

The students are enthusiastic about working together for the good of the library and their peers. They truly enjoy each other.

SURVEY ON LIBRARY SERVICES AND PROGRAMS FOR TEENS, BY LISA C. WEMETT

The same student intern who helped establish the TAB in the previous program description worked with the Teen Services Librarians to design a short survey on library services and programs to gather statistics from a sampling of students at Webster's two middle schools and two high schools. A second aspect of data gathering was to hold focus groups in each of the four schools, in order to compare and contrast answers with the survey responses. The school library media specialists provided much assistance and were especially helpful in recruiting teens for a lively focus group during study hall.

The process took approximately three months, from the development of the survey through the final report. An analysis of these two methods of data gathering were used with the new Teen Advisory Board during the following year and by the teen services librarians to guide their collection development and program offerings.

The Survey

A total of 232 surveys were completed representing grades six through eleven. The survey questions focused closely on services and programs, rather than on reading preferences. One question asked what CD the library should purchase; the responses provided significant insight into the teens' listening preferences and generated a lengthy purchase list for the audiovisual collection. The first questions dealt with the frequency of use of the public library:

- 59 percent of all teens in the sample stated they used the library at least once a month.
- 40 percent of all students indicated they use the library one time or less a year.
- 6 percent of the students use the library more than once a week.

When asked "What would make you come to the library?" the most frequent response (68 percent) was to do research for school, with well over half of each grade level indicating that was their reason for coming. Other responses included:

- 40 percent come to find a book to read for fun.
- 39 percent borrow videos or DVDs.
- 33 percent of the seventh graders come to hang out with friends.
- 40 percent of the sixth graders and 14 percent of the ninth graders come to use the café.
- 28 percent of the seventh graders and 14 percent of the sophomores come to read magazines.
- 28 percent come to use the Internet.
- 30 percent come to look for materials for personal interests (e.g., hobbies, college, and careers).
- 32 percent come to look for music CDs or tapes.

A variety of program topics were listed in the next section, stating "check any programs you would be interested in attending," so multiple responses were possible. The percentages varied widely by topic and grade level. A line was added for "my idea for a good program," which elicited many responses.

When asked "what is the best time for you to attend a program?" the students ranked the times:

- 22 percent preferred Saturday afternoon.
- 20 percent preferred weekday afternoons at 3:30 p.m.
- 19 percent preferred weekday evenings at 6:30 p.m.
- 28 percent selected "I am too busy to attend programs."

To learn if the current services for teens were being utilized, students were asked to check as many items as they wished to complete this sentence: "I have used the following library services this year." The intention of the question was also to inform the students of library services they may not have realized were available.

The ratings were as follows:

- 28 percent used a genre label on the book to locate a book they would like.

Hey! Webster Teens!

Let Your Voice Be Heard!

Please take a few moments to give the Webster Public Library your honest thoughts on the following questions:

What grade are you in? _____

Your school_____

How often do you come to the public library?

___0-1 time a year

___Once a month

___Once a week

___More than once a week

1. What would make you come to the library? (Check all that apply)

___ Find a book to read for fun

___Do research for school

___Hang out with friends

___Use the Internet

___ Look for materials for personal interests, hobbies, college/career

___Use the personal computer for word processing

___ Attend a program

___ Volunteer

___Find music CDs or tapes

___Read or borrow magazines

___Look for CD ROMs

___ Check out videos/DVDs

___ Have a snack in the café

___ Wait for a ride

___Use the photocopier

___Weather (cool in the summer, etc.)

___Other_____

2. Check any programs you would be interested in attending.

___Rubber Stamp Art

___Origami

___ Hemp jewelry

___Chess

___Fencing demonstration

___Book Discussion

___Author visit

___Internet training

___Open mike for poetry

___Teen talent night

___Theater workshop

___Martial Arts demonstration

___Term paper clinic

___Internet training (e.g. tips for search engines)

___Computer classes just for teens

My idea for a good program:

_____

3. What is the best time for you to attend a program? (rank choices by writing 1 after 1st, 2 after 2nd...)

After School: 3:30___ 4:00___

Evening: 6:30___ 7:00___

Saturday: Morning___ Afternoon___

___I am too busy to attend programs.

4. I have used the following library services this year:

___Checked library's teen web page to see what is going on

___Asked a reference question by e-mail

___Used a book list in the teen area to find something to read

___I have used labels on books (e.g., romance, humor) to locate a book I would like

___I have called the library to get help locating materials I was looking for

5. What magazine(s) would you like to see the library purchase? Circle your choices.

Asimov's Science Fiction

Teen Vogue   *BMX Plus*

Paintball   *Teen Beat*

Electronic Gaming Monthly

6. What CD would you like the library to purchase?

Artist/Group_____

Album/Title_____

7. Would you be interested in serving on a Teen Advisory Board?

Yes___ No___ Tell me more_____

Thank you!!!

If you would like to have your name entered for a drawing for a CD of your choice, fill in the blanks below:

Name:_____

Address:_____

Phone:_____

Webster Public Library
Webster Plaza, 980 Ridge Road
Webster, NY 14580
(585) 872-7075
www.websterlibrary.org

Figure 15.10 The Webster Teen survey.

- 19 percent had used a book list in the teen area to find something to read.
- 16 percent had called the library to get help locating materials.
- 7 percent had checked the teen Web page to see what was happening at the library.
- 5 percent had asked a reference question by e-mail.

The final question on the survey dealt with potential magazine purchases for the Teen Lounge. The participants were asked to choose one of six magazine titles to which the library did not subscribe.

The Focus Groups

Four focus groups were held, one in each of two middle and two high schools in the district. The best results were to hold the focus groups during study halls, when a ready audience was available. The size of the groups ranged from three to twelve students. Unlike traditional focus groups, attendance was voluntary and the school library media specialists recruited students to participate in the group. Therefore, the young adults were not a random cross-sampling of students, but teens who use the school library for study hall and the public library frequently for research.

The focus groups started with several warm-up questions concerning students' out-of-school time: things they like to do after school and on weekends, where they hang out, and activities and community groups in which they participate. These preliminary questions helped build rapport with the students and to give ideas to library staff on where to publicize future programs and services.

The next questions were similar to some that had appeared in the survey: had they been to the new library, what would cause them to go there, and how frequently did they visit? Not surprisingly, nearly every student had been to the new location. Most were wildly enthusiastic about its size and the amenities for teens—including the lounge, café, and furnishings, the number of computers, and the variety of spaces. Many commented positively about the children's area, too. As with the survey, nearly everyone said a homework assignment or major project for school would precipitate the library visit. Borrowing materials for recreation—new books, videos, DVDs, CDs, and audiobooks—was also a common response. The vast majority of the students stated they come to the library at least twice a month.

Answers to questions asked about how the students approach a reference task showed that students now consider computers the first place to start. The responses might encourage additional research in the future to determine how the library staff could better assist the students to become more productive researchers.

The students suggested having reading lists, nonfiction pathfinders on frequently asked assignments, and even a form to fill out inside the books so students could rate its value for helpful information.

When asked what suggestions they might have for the staff or what the library might loan in the future, video games were mentioned repeatedly for use on PlayStation 2, Nintendo, and Game Boy. Comics, more graphic novels, more anime videos, and loaning reference books were also suggested.

The final questions dealt with programming. It was interesting that ideas put forth in the survey were brought up without any prompting by the students in the focus groups. Ideas included a teen talent night, opportunities to work with younger children, continuation of babysitting classes, and more drawing and cartooning classes. Despite limited time, the high school students wanted to participate in book discussions and more creative arts programs like graphic arts, jewelry making, glass painting, and paper marbling.

Both the middle and high school students suggested a library lock-in where teens could spend the night in the library with a variety of activities, from hacky sack and videos to karaoke and ice cream for breakfast! Some additional creative ideas for programs included field trips, a skateboard-design workshop, a video-game tournament, and more offerings for high school students such as driver safety, college application assistance, and term-paper clinics. When asked about publicity, the usual methods seemed to work well—flyers in the library, the *Town Times*, the *TeenNews* newsletter, and word-of-mouth from parents and friends.

Many thanks were due to the student intern for her time and effort and to the school librarians for their assistance with this research method. These focus groups were a terrific opportunity to see how the library was doing, to determine if it was meeting the teen patrons' needs. Both the survey and discussions indicated it is doing well—that the new building has revitalized teen interest in the library, its resources, and the services it provides.

Lisa reports that it was great fun to talk to such a broad cross-section of the service population: from the Goth skater with the studded leather dog collar to the Pakistani junior taking multiple AP courses on her career track to medical school. All of the students were generous with their opinions, thoughtful replies, and focused comments on future program offerings.

Webster Thomas High School

Let your voice be heard!

Webster Public Library's Teen Services Department
would like your help in planning
library programs and services for teens.

9TH GRADE THROUGH 11TH GRADE
Join us for refreshments and
discussion in the school library after school

TUESDAY November 19, 2002
2:30 - 3:30 p.m.

- Express your opinions!
- Tell us how to improve the public library!
- Give us your ideas!

Please sign up with the school librarian
if you would like to come talk with us.

Thank you!

**Figure 15.11 An invitation to participate in a focus group was posted
at all the participating schools.**

**Focus Groups for Webster Public Library
Middle and High School Students**

Welcome to participants: (5min)

Help yourself to refreshments. Make a nametag tent: display example. Put your name in the middle. In the upper right corner, put the title of your favorite magazine, in the lower right corner, an animal you really like; in the upper left corner, write the name of your favorite musical group or recording artist, in the lower left corner write the name of a favorite book title, a type of book, or an author.

Introductions: (5min)

Introduce library group leaders. Group: introduce yourself and tell one thing that the group leader might like to know about you.

Explanation of intent: (2 min)

We would like your honest opinions on various questions. There are no right or wrong answers.

Everyone's opinion is important. Your answers will be confidential. We will use the information, but not put your name on the answers. We will be taking notes on the session so it is important that only one person talk at a time. Please feel free to be informal; no need to raise your hand. We will be starting a teen advisory group at the library in a few months. Your answers will help us decide how to better serve the teens in Webster.

Questions: (30 min)

1. What is your favorite thing to do outside of school?

2. Where do you like to hang out?

3. What community groups do you belong to? What after school activities are you involved in?

4. Have you been to the new library in Webster Plaza? All of our questions are focusing on what we have that is new and different at the brand new library. We want to know what you think of it and how we can make it better.

5. Why would you go to the public library? (hang out, look for magazines, borrow CDs, videos or DVDs, book to read for fun, copies to make, research, use the Internet, etc.)

6. How often do you come to the public library, if at all? (One time a year, once a month, once a week, more?)

7. Do you use the library more or less than when you were younger?

8. What do you like about the new Webster Public Library? What do you dislike?

9. When you need information for school or help with homework, where would you turn for help? Who would you ask? (Friends, teacher, school librarian, parent, public librarian, Internet, books)

Figure 15.12 The agenda and questions planned for each focus group.

Focus Groups for Webster Public Library
Middle and High School Students (*Continued*)

10. OPTIONAL: If there was a time you couldn't find what you wanted, what do you think was the reason?

11. There is a suggestion box in the new Teen Lounge. If you were there, what suggestion would you put in the box?

12 Is there something the library does not loan now that you wish that we did? (e.g., video games, board games)

13. Have you attended teen programs at the library? Why or why not?

14. What were some of the programs the library offered this fall that you heard about? Were there programs that you especially liked or were not interested in?

15. How do you find out about programs at the library? Friends, parents, newspaper, web page, school announcements, flyers

16. If you could plan any program you wanted for the library, what would you plan?

17. OPTIONAL: How do you choose a book to read? (Cover, number of pages, subject or type of book (look for stickers on the spine), author, format, recommendation, booklist)

18. OPTIONAL: What are your favorite magazines? (debrief the name tents) Who are your favorite musical groups or artists?

19. If you could have a thousand dollars to spend on something for the Webster Public Library, what would you buy?

20. What type of volunteer work have you done?

We will be starting a teen advisory group at the library in a few months. The board would help the librarians to pick out materials and plan programs that teens would like. (Give further explanation as needed.)

Distribute teen advisory board applications to those who are interested. If they decide later that they would like to apply, there are applications at the school libraries and the public library. You can use the application yourself or share it with a friend.

What personal qualities do you think would be helpful to someone on the Webster Public Library teen advisory board? How should people be selected to serve?

Thank you for sharing your ideas and opinions with us. We hope to see you at the library!

Alternate introduction:

Have kids pair up with the person next to them and find out two things they didn't know about that person, and make a name tent with that person's name to put in front of the person. Each person will introduce the person they talked with and tell what they found out.

Figure 15.12 (*Continued*)

Appendix A

The Questionnaire

This is the questionnaire sent to the young adult librarians who responded to the requests for successful teen programs.

101 MORE TEEN PROGRAMS THAT WORK QUESTIONNAIRE

Greetings!

Young adult librarians like you are creating wonderful programs for the teens in your communities. I would like to give you an opportunity to share your favorite programs with others in a new book to be published by Neal-Schuman Publishers, Inc. in 2005. *101 More Teen Programs that Work* will be a collection of your programs and successes. This questionnaire will help make sure the program description will be complete so others can try it.

Part one: Your contact information

1. Your name
2. Your title
3. Your e-mail address
4. Your library
5. Library address
6. Library phone
7. Library fax

Part two: Your program

1. What did you name your program?
2. Who was your intended audience?
3. When was your program (date and time, occasion)?
4. How long was your program?
5. Where was your program held?

6. Describe your program. Include the sequence of events.
7. Did you make a Collection Connection during the program?
8. What special materials are needed to do this program? Are there special resources?
9. How many staff members and/or volunteers are needed?
10. What were your expenses? Who funds your teen programs?
11. How did you publicize your program?
12. Did you get any feedback from the teens after your program? Do you have any quotes to share?
13. Did you have handouts for the program you would like to share?
14. Do you have photos of the program to share?

Please send your responses to me via snail mail or e-mail.
Thank you for sharing your work with other libraries!

RoseMary Honnold
honnolro@oplin.org
Coshocton Public Library
655 Main St.
Coshocton, OH 43812
740-622-0956 ext. 14, Fax: 740-622-4331

Appendix B

The Contributors

This book would not be possible without the generosity of the young adult librarians who devote their time and energy to creating programs that work with teens at their home libraries. The following contributors shared their work for this book:

Amy Ackerman, Reference Librarian
aackerma@martin.fl.us
Martin County Library System
2351 SE Monterey Road, Stuart, FL 34996
772-221-1413, Fax: 772-221-1358

Mary Adamowski, Assistant Head of Youth Services
adamowskimoppl@yahoo.com
Orland Park Public Library
14760 Park Lane, Orland Park, IL 60462
708-349-8138, Fax: 708-349-8196

Mamie C. Alsdurf, Library Student
Columbus, OH

Susan G. Barhan, Children's Librarian
sbarhan@imcpl.lib.in.us
Shelby Branch of Indianapolis Marion County Public Library
2502 Shelby, Indianapolis, IN 46227
317-784-4084

Vickie Beene-Beavers, Young Adult Librarian
vbbeene@af.public.lib.ga.us

Ponce de Leon Branch
980 Ponce de Leon Avenue, Atlanta, GA
404-885-7821, Fax: 404-885-7822

Deb Belew, Library Assistant II
belewde@oplin.org
Minerva Public Library
677 Lynnwood Drive, Minerva, OH 44657
330-868-4101, Fax: 330-868-4267

Rhonda Belyea, Youth Services Librarian
rbelyea@crrl.org
Central Rappahannock Regional Library
1201 Caroline Street, Fredericksburg, VA 22401
540-372-1144, Fax: 540-899-9941

Anthony Bernier, Ph.D., Director, Teen Services
ABernier@OaklandLibrary.org
Oakland Public Library
125 14th Street, Oakland, CA 94611
510-238-3850, Fax: 510- 238-2232

Spring Lea Henry, Youth Librarian
slboehler@dclibraries.org
Philip S. Miller Library
100 S. Wilcox Street, Castle Rock, CO 80104
303-688-7700, Fax: 303-688-7715

Christine Borne, Reference Librarian
Shaker Heights Public Library
16500 Van Aken Boulevard, Shaker Heights, OH 44120
216-991-2030, Fax: 216-991-5951

Sophie R. Brookover, Youth Services Librarian
sophie@mtlaurel.lib.nj.us
Mount Laurel Library
100 Walt Whitman Avenue, Mount Laurel, NJ 08054
856-234-7319, Fax: 856-234-6916

Nicolas Brown, Teen Advisory Council President
nickbrown2k2@earthlink.net

Corona Public Library
650 S. Main Street, Corona, CA 92882
909-736-2387

Dana Burton, Coordinator, Teen Services
dburton@monroe.lib.in.us
Monroe County Public Library
303 E. Kirkwood Avenue, Bloomington, IN 47408
812-349-3050 ext 2055, Fax: 812-349-3051

Randee J. Bybee, Library Assistant
RBybee@ci.upland.ca.us
Upland Public Library
450 N. Euclid Avenue, Upland, CA 91786
909-931-4213, Fax: 909-931-4209

Jan Chapman, Youth Librarian
jchapman@ascpl.lib.oh.us
Akron-Summit County Public Library/Norton Branch
3930 S. Cleve-Mass Road, Norton, OH 44203
330-825-7800, Fax: 330-825-5155

Donna Childs, Young Adult Librarian
DChilds@mailserv.mvlc.lib.ma.us
Newburyport Public Library
94 State Street, Newburyport, MA 01950
978-465-4428 ext 228, Fax: 978-463-0394

Laura Cleveland, Youth Services Librarian
lcleveland@cowtx.org
Watauga Public Library
7109 Whitley Road, Watauga, TX 76148
817-514-5866, Fax: 817-581-3910

Joanne Coker, Youth Services Coordinator
cokerjo@oplin.org
Mary L. Cook Public Library
381 Old Stage Road, Waynesville, OH 45068
513-897-4826

Aiesha Collins, First Assistant, Teen Services
acollins@starklibrary.org
Stark County District Library
715 Market Avenue North, Canton, OH 44702
330-452-0665, Fax: 330-458-2650

Karen Cruze, Youth Services Librarian
kcruze@nsls.info
Northbrook Public Library
1201 Cedar Lane, Northbrook, IL 60062
847-272-6224, Fax: 847-272-5362

Kristina Daily, Adult Services Manager
kdaily@champaign.org
Champaign Public Library
505 S. Randolph Street, Champaign, IL 61820
217-403-2070, Fax: 217-403-2073

Suzanne Daveluy, Librarian II, Co-coordinator Teen Services
suzy.daveluy@ci.stockton.ca.us
Stockton-San Joaquin County Public Library, Cesar Chavez Central Library
605 N. El Dorado Street, Stockton, CA 95202
209-937-8221, Fax: 209-937-8547

Karen J. DeAngelo, Youth Services Librarian
Kdeangelo@sals.edu
Town of Ballston Community Library
2 Lawmar Lane, Burnt Hills, NY 12027
518-399-8174, Fax: 518-399-8187

Bonnie Demarchi, Regional Teen Services Manager
Bdemarchi@Cuyahoga.lib.oh.us
Cuyahoga County Public Library
7335 Ridge Road, Parma, OH 44129
440-885-5362, Fax: 440-885-2105

Denise DiPaolo, Young Adult Librarian
ddipaolo@suffolk.lib.ny.us
Rogers Memorial Library
91 Coopers Farm Road, Southampton, NY 11968
631-283-0774 ext 548, Fax: 631-287-6539

Amy E. Doty, Young Adult Librarian/Head of Circulation
dotyam@oplin.org
Martins Ferry Public Library
20 James Wright Place, Martins Ferry, OH 43935
740-633-0314, Fax: 740-633-0935

Olivia S. Durant, Teen Services Librarian
odurant@mcls.rochester.lib.ny.us
Webster Public Library
Webster Plaza, 980 Ridge Road, Webster, NY 14580
585-872-7075 ext 113, Fax: 585-872-7073

Kara Falck, Children's/Teen Librarian
falckk@einetwork.net
Shaler North Hills Library
1822 Mt. Royal Boulevard, Glenshaw, PA 15116
412-486-0211, Fax: 412-486-8286

Lora Fegley, Head of Youth Services
lfegley@martin.fl.us
Martin County Library System
2351 S.E. Monterey Road, Stuart, FL 34996
772-221-1413, Fax: 772-221-1358

Kristin Fletcher-Spear, Young Adult Librarian
kfletcher-spear@glendaleaz.com
Glendale Public Library System, Foothills Branch Library
19055 North 57th Avenue, Glendale, AZ 85382
623-930-3840, Fax: 623-930-3855

Lin Flores, Senior Librarian-Reference and Youth Services
lflore@camden.lib.nj.us
South County Regional Library
35 Coopers Folly Road, Atco, NJ 08004
856-753-2537, Fax: 856-753-7289

Jennifer Garner, Assistant Director/Teen Librarian
jgarner@north-liberty.lib.ia.us
North Liberty Community Library
520 W. Cherry Street, P.O. Box 320, North Liberty, IA 52317
319-626-5701, Fax: 319-626-5733

Cynthia Gaynor, Head of Reference
refreed@oplin.org
Rood Memorial Library
167 E. Main Street, Ravenna, OH 44266
330-296-2827, Fax: 330-296-3780

Tina Gentile, Library Assistant, Children Services
tgentile@cml.oh.us
Columbus Metropolitan Library, New Albany Branch
200 Market Street, New Albany, OH 43045
614-724-2540, Fax: 614-724-2549

Ed Goldberg
longislandlibrarian@yahoo.com
Syosset Public Library
225 S. Oyster Bay Road, Syosset, NY 11791
516-921-7161

Janet Good, Young Adult Librarian
janetg@co.summit.co.us
North Branch Library, Summit County Library
P.O. Box 1248, Silverthorne, CO 80498
970-468-5887, Fax: 970-513-0854

Gretchen H. Hanley, Reference/Young Adult Librarian
gretchhy@lori.state.ri.us
Lincoln Public Library
145 Old River Road, Lincoln, RI 02865
401-333-2422, Fax: 401-333-4154

Nancy Heuser, Young Adult Librarian Assistant
Heuseroppl@yahoo.com
Orland Park Public Library
14760 Park Lane, Orland Park, IL 60462
708-349-8138, Fax: 708-349-8196

Cathy Hochadel, YA Services Representative
Bu_cathy@dayton.lib.oh.us
Dayton Metro Library, Burkhart Branch
4680 Burkhardt Avenue, Dayton, OH 45431
937-227-9503, Fax: 937-256-5199

Susanna Holstein, Branch Services Manager
susanna.holstein@kanawha.lib.wv.us
Kanawha County Public Library System
123 Capitol Street, Charleston, WV 25301
304-343-4646 ext 291

Chris Holt, Branch Manager
chris.holt@cincinnatilibrary.org
Monfort Heights Branch, Public Library of Cincinnati and Hamilton County
3825 West Fork Road, Cincinnati, OH 45247
513-369-4472, Fax: 513-369-4473

Amy C. Hoptay, Teen Services Librarian
mamahopper@verizon.net
Sewickley Public Library
500 Thorn Street, Sewickley, PA 15143
412-741-6920, Fax: 412-741-6099

Trish Hull, Youth Services Librarian
thull@slco.lib.ut.us
Kearns Library
5350 South 4220 West, Kearns, UT 84118
801-944-7612, Fax: 801-967-8958

Patrick Jones, Consultant
patrick@connecting.com
www.connectingya.com

Amy Korpieski, Youth Services Librarian
akorpieski@gcpl.lib.oh.us
Greene County Public Library, Xenia
76 E. Market Street, Xenia, OH 45385
937-376-2995 ext 330, Fax: 937-376-5523

Sandra Lang, Young Adult Librarian
langsa@oplin.org
Louisville Public Library
700 Lincoln Avenue, Louisville, OH 44641
330-875-1696

Kelly Laszczak, Young Adult Librarian
klaszczak@hinsdale.lib.il.us
Hinsdale Public Library
20 E. Maple Street, Hinsdale, IL 60521
630-986-1976, Fax: 630-986-9720

Ira Lax, Outreach Assistant
Laxi@aadl.org
Ann Arbor District Library
343 S. Fifth Avenue, Ann Arbor, MI 48104
734-327-8365, Fax: 734-327-8355

Audrey Leventhal, Teen Librarian
aleventhal@shakerlibrary.org
Shaker Heights Public Library
16500 Van Aken Boulevard, Shaker Heights, OH 44120
216-991-2030, Fax: 216-991-5951

Sharon Macdonald, Director of Youth Services
sharon@rye.lib.nh.us
Rye Public Library
581 Washington Road, Rye, NH 03870
603-964-8401, Fax: 603-964-7065

Mark A. Malcolm, Children's /YA Librarian
mmalcolm@minlib.net
Maynard Public Library
197 Main Street, Maynard, MA 01754
978-897-1010, Fax: 978-897-9884

Jody Maples, Youth Services Manager
jlmaples@lpld.lib.in.us
Lawrenceburg Public Library District
123 West High Street, Lawrenceburg, IN 47025
812-537-2775, Fax: 812-537-2810

Jennifer R. McIntosh, Young Adult Librarian/Webmistress
mcintoshj@uhls.lib.ny.us
East Greenbush Community Library
10 Community Way, East Greenbush, NY 12061
518-477-7476 ext 105

Ann Melrose, Youth Services Librarian
amelrose@hclib.org
Hennepin County Library
12601 Ridgedale Drive, Minnetonka, MN 55305
952-847-8500, Fax: 952-847-8600

Alison Miller, Youth Services Coordinator
millera@stls.org
Dundee Library
32 Water Street, Dundee, NY 14837
607-243-5938, Fax: 607-243-7733

Heather E. Miller, Young Adult Specialist
hmiller@bham.lib.al.us
Homewood Public Library
1721 Oxmoor Road, Homewood, AL 35209
205-877-8661, Fax: 205-802-6424

Sharon Moynes, Senior Librarian, Circ/Browsery/Gateway/Hub
smoynes@tpl.toronto.on.ca
North York Central Library
5120 Yonge Street, Toronto, Ontario M2N 5N9
416-395-5784

Karissa A. Murphy, Young Adult Librarian
karissa_ann5@yahoo.com
Bucyrus Public Library
200 East Mansfield Street, Bucyrus, OH 44820
419-562-7327, Fax: 419-562-7437

Ria Newhouse, Teen Services Librarian
rnewhouse@hancockpub.lib.in.us
Hancock County Public Library
700 North Broadway, Greenfield, IN 46140
317-462-5141 ext 25, Fax: 317-462-5711

Janet Oneacre, Library Assistant I
jankayo@aol.com
Minerva Public Library
677 Lynnwood Drive, Minerva, OH 44657
330-868-4101, Fax: 330-868-4267

Jill Patterson, Branch Manager
jkpatterson@ocpl.org
La Habra Branch Library/Orange County Public Library
221 E. La Habra Boulevard, La Habra, CA 90631
562-694-0078, Fax: 562-691-8043

Miriam Perez, Librarian
MPerez2@ci.santa-ana.ca.us
Santa Ana Public Library
26 Civic Center Plaza, Santa Ana, CA 92701
714-647-5258

Melissa Pillot, Young Adult Specialist
mpillot@slpl.lib.mo.us
St. Louis Public Library
1301 Olive, St. Louis, MO 63103
314-539-0389

Rebecca Purdy, Youth Services Manager
rpurdy@crrl.org
Central Rappahannock Regional Library
1201 Caroline Street, Fredericksburg, VA 22401
540-372-1144 ext 246, Fax: 540-899-9941

Karen Reed
Glendale Public Library System, Foothills Branch Library
19055 North 57th Avenue, Glendale, AZ 85382
623-930-3840, Fax: 623-930-3855

Carrie Robertson, Teen Library Assistant
cirobertson@ocpl.org
La Habra Branch Library/Orange County Public Library
221 E. La Habra Boulevard, La Habra, CA 90631
562-694-0078, Fax: 562-691-8043

Joanne Rode, Young Adult Librarian
jorode@ocpl.org
Laguna Niguel Library
30341 Crown Valley Parkway, Laguna Niguel, CA 92677
949-249-5252, Fax: 949-249-5258

Leah Ducato Rudolph, Information Services Librarian
lrudolph@albright.org
Abington Community Library
1200 W. Grove Street, Clarks Summit, PA 18411
570-587-3440, Fax: 570-587-3809

Irene Scherer, Asst. Head of Public Services
ischerer@rla.lib.il.us
Round Lake Area Library
906 Hart Road, Round Lake, IL 60073
847-546-7060, Fax: 847-546-7104

Virginia Schonwald, Children's/YA Librarian
Virginia@metrocast.net
Barrington Public Library
39 Province Lane, Barrington, NH 03825
603-664-9715, Fax: 603-664-5219

Andrea Schimpf
Bucyrus Public Library
200 East Mansfield Street
Bucyrus, OH 44820
419-562-7327, Fax: 419-562-7437

Margie Walker, YA Librarian
mwalker@mvlc.org
Amesbury Public Library
149 Main Street, Amesbury, MA 01913
978-388-8148, Fax: 978-388-2662

Elise Sheppard, Teen Librarian
Elise.J.Sheppard@nhmccd.edu
Cy-Fair College Branch Library, Harris County Public Library
9191 Barker Cypress Road, Cypress, TX 77433
281-290-5248, Fax: 281-290-5288

Paula Shockley, Teen Library Assistant
pshockley@cml.lib.oh.us
Gahanna Branch, Columbus Metropolitan Libraries
310 Granville Street, Gahanna, OH 43230
614-645-2270, Fax: 614-645-2279

Melissa Sillitoe, Librarian
msillito@mail.slcpl.lib.ut.us
Salt Lake City Public Library, Chapman Branch
577 South 900 West, Salt Lake City, UT 84104
801-594-8623

Brian Simons, Librarian
bsimons@mcls.lib.wi.us
Manitowoc Public Library
707 Quay Street, Manitowoc, WI 54220
920-683-4863, Fax: 920-683-4873

Jennifer Singell-Thanasiu, Young Adult Coordinator
jthanasiu@cvrls.net
Chattahoochee Valley Regional Library System
1120 Bradley Drive, Columbus, GA 31906-2800
706-649-0780 ext 118, Fax: 706-649-1914

Debbie Socha, Library Assistant
storyladydebbie@yahoo.com
Geauga West Library
13455 Chillicothe Road, Chesterland, OH 44026
440-729-2014, Fax: 440-729-7517

Beth Solomon, Technical Information Librarian, Wired for Youth Librarian
beth.solomon@ci.austin.tx.us
Southeast Austin Community Branch, Austin Public Library
5803 Nuckols Crossing Road, Austin, TX 78744
512-462-1452, Fax: 512-447-7639

Amanda Spargo, Adult and Children's Services Assistant
Amanda.Spargo@library.ottawa.on.ca
Ottawa Public Library, Ruth E. Dickinson Branch
100 Malvern Drive, Ottawa, Ontario K2J 2G5
613-580-2796, Fax: 613-825-3500

Linda Staskus, Children's Librarian
Parma-Ridge Branch, Cuyahoga County Public Library
5850 Ridge Road, Parma, OH 44129
440-888-4300, Fax: 440-884-2097

Jennifer Stencel, Youth Librarian
jstencel@ascpl.lib.oh.us
Richfield Branch Library, Akron-Summit County Public Library System
3761 S. Grant Street, P.O. Box 287, Richfield, OH 44286
330-659-4343, Fax: 330-659-6205

Shannan Sword, Teen Services Librarian
s.sword@lanepl.org
Lane Public Library, Fairfield Branch
1485 Corydale Drive, Fairfield, OH 45014
513-858-3238 ext 317, Fax: 513-858-3298

Lola Teubert, Young Adult/Literacy Services Librarian
lolat@evpl.org
Evansville Vanderburgh Public Library
22 SE Fifth Street, Evansville, IN 47708
812-428-8225, Fax: 812-428-8215

Lisa Tharp, Librarian II-Lead
lisa.tharp@phxlib.org
Phoenix Public Library, Palo Verde Branch
4402 N. 51st Avenue, Phoenix, AZ 85031
602-262-6806, Fax: 602-261-8455

Diane Tuccillo, Librarian III/Young Adult Coordinator
diane.tuccillo@cityofmesa.org
City of Mesa Library
64 E. First Street, Mesa, AZ 85201
480-644-2735, Fax: 480-644-3490

Phyllis Uchrin, Head of Youth Services
puchrin@dunedinfl.net
Dunedin Public Library
223 Douglas Avenue, Dunedin, FL 34698
727-298-3080, Fax: 727-298-3088

Linda Uhler, Teen Services Associate
luhler@holmeslib.org
Holmes County District Public Library
3102 Glen Drive, Millersburg, OH 44654
330-674-5972, Fax: 330-674-1938

Laura Vinograd, Youth Librarian
lvinogra@mail.win.org
Spencer Road Branch Library
427 Spencer Road, St. Peters, MO 63376
636-447-2320, Fax: 636-926-3948

Eva Volin
Stockton-San Joaquin County Public Library, Cesar Chavez Central Library
605 N. El Dorado Street, Stockton, CA 95202
209-937-8221, Fax: 209-937-8547

Jeni Venker Weidenbenner, Reference and Technology Librarian
jvweidenbenner@htls.lib.il.us
Bourbonnais Public Library
250 W. John Casey Road, Bourbonnais, IL 60914
815-933-1727, Fax: 815-933-1961

Joan Weiskotten, Youth Services Librarian
Clifton Park-Halfmoon Public Library
47 Clifton Country Road, Clifton Park, NY 12065
518-371-8622, Fax: 518-371-3799

Lisa C. Wemett, Assistant Director for Reference and Teen Services
lwemett@mcls.rochester.lib.ny.us
Webster Public Library
Webster Plaza, 980 Ridge Road, Webster, NY 14580
585-872-7075 ext 111, Fax: 585-872-7073

Carly Wiggins, Assistant Branch Manager/Young Adult Librarian
cwiggins@acpl.lib.in.us
Allen County Public Library, Tecumseh Branch Library
1411 East State Boulevard, Fort Wayne, IN 46805
260-421-1360, Fax: 260-482-5236

Theresa Wordelmann, Young Adult Librarian
theword@lmxac.org
Old Bridge Public Library
One Old Bridge Plaza, Old Bridge, NJ 08857
732-721-5600 ext 5044, Fax: 732-607-0436

Lara M. Zeises, Young Adult Author
zeisgeist@aol.com

Index

About the Author

RoseMary Honnold is the Young Adult Services Coordinator at Coshocton Public Library in Coshocton, Ohio. RoseMary is the creator of the "See YA Around" Web site at www.cplrmh.com and the author of *101+ Teen Programs that Work* and coauthor of *Serving Seniors: A How-To-Do-It Manual for Librarians*. RoseMary has presented several conference sessions and workshops on young adult and senior adult programming in libraries. Besides working, writing, reading, and painting, RoseMary enjoys spending time with her family.